Lecture Notes
in Economics and
Mathematical Systems

Managing Editors: M. Beckmann and W. Krelle

363

Clemens Puppe

Distorted Probabilities and Choice under Risk

Springer-Verlag
Berlin Heidelberg New York London Paris
Tokyo Hong Kong Barcelona Budapest

Managing Editors

Prof. Dr. M. Beckmann
Brown University
Providence, RI 02912, USA

Prof. Dr. W. Krelle
Institut für Gesellschafts- und Wirtschaftswissenschaften
der Universität Bonn
Adenauerallee 24–42, D-5300 Bonn, FRG

Author

Clemens Puppe
Institut für Statistik und Mathematische Wirtschaftstheorie
Universität Karlsruhe, Rechenzentrum
Zirkel 2, D-7500 Karlsruhe 1, FRG

ISBN 3-540-54247-7 Springer-Verlag Berlin Heidelberg New York
ISBN 0-387-54247-7 Springer-Verlag New York Berlin Heidelberg

Printed in Germany

Printing and binding: Druckhaus Beltz, Hemsbach/Bergstr.
2142/3140-543210 – Printed on acid-free paper

In memoriam

PROF. DR. RUDOLF HENN
9.11.1922 - 18.11.1989

Acknowledgement

I am very grateful to Professor P. Kischka for all the stimulating and inspiring conversations we had during the last years.
I also wish to thank Professor G. Bol and Professor W. Eichhorn for helpful comments.
Karlsruhe, May 1991 Clemens Puppe

Contents

Introduction 1

1 Axiomatic Utility Theory under Risk 8

1.1 Historical Overview 9

1.2 The Axiomatic Basis of Expected Utility Theory 14

1.3 The Empirical Evidence against the Independence Axiom 20

1.4 Non-Linear Utility Theory under Risk 23

1.4.1 Weighted Linear Utility Theory 23

1.4.2 Theories with the Betweenness Property 26

1.4.3 Anticipated Utility Theory 28

1.4.4 The Dual Theory 30

1.4.5 The General Rank-Dependent Utility Model . . 32

1.4.6 Implicit Rank-Linear Utility Theory 37

2 A Rank-Dependent Utility Model with Prize-Dependent Distortion of Probabilities 40

2.1 Rank-Dependent Utility Theory Reconsidered 42

2.1.1 The Generalized Utility Function 42

2.1.2 Absolute Continuity 45

2.1.3 The Set of Elementary Lotteries 49

2.2 Homogeneity on Elementary Lotteries 50

2.2.1 The Common Ratio Effect 52

2.2.2 The Allais Paradox 53

2.3 Further Evidence for Prize-Dependent Distortions of Probabilities 55
2.4 A Characterization Theorem 56
2.5 Rank-Dependent Utility Theory and Relative Utility . 58
2.6 A Generalized Model 62

3 Risk Aversion **67**
3.1 Risk Aversion in the General Rank-Dependent Utility Model 69
3.2 Risk Aversion and Homogeneity 75
3.3 Decreasing Risk Aversion 80
3.4 The Friedman-Savage Hypothesis 82

Conclusion **88**

References **92**

Introduction

During the development of modern probability theory in the 17th century it was commonly held that the attractiveness of a gamble offering the payoffs $x_1, ..., x_n$ with probabilities $p_1, ..., p_n$ is given by its *expected value* $\sum_1^n x_i p_i$. Accordingly, the decision problem of choosing among different such gambles – which will be called *prospects* or *lotteries* in the sequel – was thought to be solved by maximizing the corresponding expected values.

The famous *St.Petersburg paradox* posed by Nicholas Bernoulli in 1728, however, conclusively demonstrated the fact that individuals consider more than just the expected value.[1] The resolution of the St.Petersburg paradox was proposed independently by Gabriel Cramer and Nicholas's cousin Daniel Bernoulli [BERNOULLI 1738/1954]. Their argument was that in a gamble with payoffs x_i the decisive factors are not the payoffs themselves but their *subjective values* $u(x_i)$. According to this argument gambles are evaluated on the basis of the expression $\sum_1^n u(x_i)p_i$. This hypothesis – with a somewhat different interpretation of the function u – has been given a solid axiomatic foundation in 1944 by v.Neumann and Morgenstern and is now known as the *expected utility hypothesis*. The resulting model has served for a long time as the preeminent theory of choice under risk, especially in its economic applications.

At present there is, however, a growing dissatisfaction with this model due to repeatedly accumulated evidence against the expected utility hypothesis (see sections 1.1 and 1.3). One direction of recent research work suggests to explain this evidence in terms of *"distorted" probabilities.*

[1] A detailed historical overview of the discussion caused by the St.Petersburg paradox can be found in [Jorland 1987].

The idea that decision makers when confronted with choices between risky prospects distort given probabilities, i.e. transform the probabilities into "decision weights", is not new (see e.g. [EDWARDS 1955, 1962], [FELLNER 1961], [HANDA 1977], [KARMARKAR 1978], [KAHNEMAN AND TVERSKY 1979]). It is a natural extension of Bernoulli's hypothesis that not the given amounts of money but rather their utilities are relevant for a decision maker.

But it was not until 1982 that this idea has been made operational in a normatively appealing model of choice under risk by QUIGGIN [1982]. The essential characteristic of his model distinguishing it from former approaches is that the decision maker does not transform single probabilities but the probability distribution as a whole and maximizes the expected utility with respect to the transformed probability distribution on the set of outcomes. Thus, the transformed measure assigns to each outcome in a lottery a certain decision weight depending on the whole lottery.

However, in Quiggins approach – which he called *anticipated utility theory* and which is now also known as *expected utility theory with rank-dependent probabilities* – the decision weights are not affected by changes of the outcomes which preserve their ranking in the outcome space. The following example shows that this may be a serious restriction.

Suppose that an individual with linear utility of money[2] prefers a sure gain of 5$ to the lottery promising 500$ with probability 0.01 and 0$ with probability 0.99. The reason for her choice could be that she is hungry and wants to buy a 5$-meal rather than to hope that she would receive the 500$. Suppose furthermore that she would prefer at the same time a 0.01 chance of getting 50000$ (and 0$ otherwise)

---

[2]The argument does not depend on this specific form of the utility of money which is assumed here only for simplicity. However, the specific data in the example *do* depend on the shape of the utility function. For a thorough discussion of the issue raised by the above example see section 2.3.

to the sure gain of 500$ because she finds it exciting to gamble for 50000$ and thinks that this is worth 500$ (and staying hungry).

Obviously, in this example the outcomes corresponding to the probability 0.01 have the same rank in the lottery to which they belong. According to anticipated utility theory the decision weight attached to the probability 0.01 should therefore be the same in both lotteries. But such an individual cannot admit a constant decision weight $f(0.01)$ for the probability 0.01 since her first choice implies $f(0.01) < 0.01$ and her second choice implies $f(0.01) > 0.01$. On the other hand, there seems to be nothing wrong or *irrational* with the behavior described in this example.[3]

The explanation of the above described behavior which will be proposed here is that the decision weight which an individual attaches to the probability of winning a certain amount of money is not independent of this amount even if its rank is preserved in a given lottery.[4] More specifically, it will be argued that small probabilities are disproportionately overweighted when the corresponding prizes become high. This hypothesis yields a plausible explanation not only of the example above but also of the generally observed inclination of many people to participate in lotteries promising high prizes with a very small probability.

The main idea lying behind our approach to decision making under risk can be best understood by firstly restricting attention to the subset of *elementary lotteries*. This set consists of all lotteries with only two outcomes one of which is always 0 (or more generally the "status quo"). Denoting the other outcome by x and its probability

[3]It should be emphasized that an individual with such an attitude towards risk is *risk averse* at low outcome levels and *risk seeking* at high outcome levels (see chapter 3, especially section 3.4).

[4]For a similar explanation of empirical observations which arise in the context of uncertainty rather than risk see [Hazen 1987].

by p, an expected utility maximizer can be represented on this set by an utility functional v which is *linear* in p, i.e. $v(x,p) = u(x)p$.

The anticipated utility model generalizes the expected utility model by implying a representation of the form $v(x,p) = u(x)f(p)$ for some strictly increasing transformation function $f : [0,1] \to [0,1]$. Note that in this representation the transformation of the probability p does not depend on the involved amount x, thus maintaining the multiplicative separability of the expected utility representation. Therefore, the anticipated utility approach is not compatible with the behavior described by the example above.

The approach taken here focuses on another property of the expected utility representation which does not exclude the kind of behavior described above, namely the *homogeneity* in the probability p. The most general representation of preferences among elementary lotteries which maintains the homogeneity in the probability p takes the form $v(x,p) = u(x)p^{g(x)}$ for some real-valued function g. Formally, in this representation $g(x)$ is the degree of homogeneity of v with respect to p given x. On the other hand, g can be interpreted as a function which *distorts the probability p depending on the outcome x*. Thus, the resulting model incorporates in a simple manner the idea of prize-dependent transformations of probabilities and is therefore compatible with the kind of behavior described in the example above.

It will be proved that the hypothesis of homogeneity in the probability can also serve as a plausible explanation of other observed behavioral patterns like the well-known Allais paradox and the common ratio effect. The fact that small probabilities are disproportionately overweighted when prizes become high follows in the homogeneous model from a stochastic dominance argument. Therefore, the homogeneous model captures in some way an *optimistic* attitude towards gambling.

In its general form homogeneity in the probability p is of course not compatible with the *independence axiom* of expected utility theory, but it is compatible with a weaker principle, the so-called *ordinal independence axiom*, which was recently suggested as a normatively appealing alternative to the independence axiom (see [GREEN AND JULLIEN 1988], [SEGAL 1989]). The class of models in which preferences satisfy ordinal independence are subsumed under the name of *rank-dependent utility (henceforth RDU) theory.* Special cases of this approach are the anticipated utility model, the *dual theory* of YAARI [1987] and the expected utility model.

Extending preferences that admit a homogeneous representation on the set of elementary lotteries by means of the ordinal independence principle to the set of all distributions gives rise to another specialization of the RDU approach. The resulting model will be referred to as the *homogeneous RDU model*. A characterization theorem for the homogeneous RDU model is obtained by using a certain numerical index which will be called the *relative utility index.* As a further application of this index new characterizations of the anticipated utility model, the dual theory and the expected utility model will be given in terms of relative utility.

Our analysis will show that all the above mentioned models imply strong behavioral restrictions reflected by specific shapes of the relative utility index. Therefore, also a more general model which does not assume a specific form of the relative utility index will be examined. This general model contains both the anticipated utility model and the homogeneous RDU model as special cases.

An important feature of a theory of choice under risk are the conditions under which an individual will display *risk aversion.* It turns out that the homogeneous RDU model is very sensitive to the specific formulation of risk aversion which is applied. It will be shown that, in general, homogeneity is incompatible with a strong concept of risk aversion. However, as one of our main results in this context we will prove that although the homogeneous RDU model implies a kind of optimism towards gambling it is still compatible with a weaker notion of risk aversion even if there is no diminishing marginal utility of wealth. This fact has important implications for the flexibility of the homogeneous RDU model as a descriptive theory of behavior in the presence of risk. In particular, it will be shown that this model is consistent with (and in some cases predicts) the behavior described in connection with the *Friedman-Savage hypothesis.*

We will proceed as follows. Chapter 1 reviews the axiomatic basis of the expected utility model and surveys the observed violations of one of its fundamental principles, the independence axiom. Also the most important alternative theories of choice under risk suggested as a reaction to the evidence against the independence axiom are formally treated there.

In chapter 2 the homogeneous RDU model is developed and analyzed. The first section collects some results concerning the general RDU model which are not available in the literature but which are of importance for our approach. Section 2.2 is devoted to the homogeneous version of the RDU model. It is demonstrated how it explains the empirical patterns discussed in section 1.3. Some general considerations concerning prize-dependent distortions of probabilities versus uniform distortions of probabilities are gathered in section 2.3. The characterization theorem for the homogeneous RDU model is proved in section 2.4. In section 2.5 the method developed in 2.4 is applied to characterize other specializations of the general RDU approach. Finally, the aforementioned generalization of the homogeneous RDU model is examined in section 2.6.

Chapter 3 investigates the impact of the concept of risk aversion on the general RDU model (section 3.1) and especially on the homogeneous version of it (section 3.2). The two final sections contain some further remarks on the notion of *decreasing risk aversion* (section 3.3) and a discussion of the Friedman-Savage hypothesis within the framework of the homogeneous RDU model (section 3.4).

Chapter 1

Axiomatic Utility Theory under Risk

This chapter reviews the developments of the theory of choice under risk since v.NEUMANN and MORGENSTERN [1947] presented the first axiomatic formulation of the expected utility model. The purpose of this review is to set the stage for the investigations of the following chapters and to give the context of the problems treated there.

Section 1.1 gives a short historical overview of the debate about the expected utility paradigm which has now led many researchers to abandon or at least weaken some of the principles of expected utility theory. Emphasis is on those proposals that deal with distortions of probabilities. Section 1.2 introduces the formal framework of our analysis along with some notation. A version of the expected utility theorem adapted to this framework is also stated there. The empirical evidence against expected utility maximizing behavior is briefly described in section 1.3 where the focus is on the evidence concerning the *linearity in the probabilities.* There are several axiomatic utility theories designed to accomodate behavior indicating that probabilities are handled in a non-linear way. These theories are presented in section 1.4.

1.1 Historical Overview

Ever since its axiomatic foundation by v.Neumann and Morgenstern in the case of pure risk and by SAVAGE [1954] in the case of uncertainty[1] the expected utility hypothesis has played a dominant role in the economic analysis of risk and uncertainty. Still it is the most widely applied theory in many fields of economics. However, the early criticism of the expected utility paradigm put forward (among others) by ALLAIS [1953] and ELLSBERG [1961] has been strongly confirmed by extensive empirical investigations in the seventies. Researchers such as MACCRIMMON [1968], LICHTENSTEIN and SLOVIC [1973], SLOVIC and TVERSKY [1974], MACCRIMMON and LARSSON [1979], GRETHER and PLOTT [1979], KAHNEMAN and TVERSKY [1979] have found that the principles of expected utility theory are indeed *systematically* violated (see also [MACHINA 1987] for a survey of the empirical data concerning choice under risk and uncertainty). The empirical evidence reported in those investigations therefore cast serious doubt not only on the *descriptive* content of the expected utility hypothesis but also on the claim that *rational* decision makers should always obey the axioms of expected utility theory.[2] Consequently, there has been a growing interest in alternative models of preferences under risk and uncertainty which were more satisfactory from a descriptive point of view but which would on the other hand not give up too much of the normative appeal and the mathematical elegance of the expected utility model. Since the beginning of the eighties a considerable amount

[1]The terms "risk" and "uncertainty" refer to the Knightian distinction between decision situations whith known and unknown probabilities.

[2]It seems to be an interesting question in this context whether a set of behavioral postulates can be acceptable from a *normative* viewpoint even if these postulates are systematically violated by most decision makers. I believe the answer to this question is no, but there are of course other positions (see e.g. [Savage 1954], [Raiffa 1961] and [Schneeweiß 1967]).

of such alternative theories has been proposed by both economists and mathematical psychologists.

The set of models with a significant normative interest – as opposed to those with a more descriptive intention – can be classified by the manner in which the axioms of expected utility theory are weakened (see also [Weber and Camerer 1987], [Fishburn 1988], [Karni and Schmeidler 1990], [Kischka and Puppe 1991] for surveys of these proposals). The three core axioms of expected utility theory are

- an order axiom, i.e. completeness and transitivity of preferences,
- some kind of continuity requirement ensuring the existence of a real-valued representation of the preferences, and
- a separability condition which is known as the *independence axiom* in the case of pure risk and as the *sure thing principle* in the case of uncertainty.

Besides some early models which abandon the completeness assumption or continuity requirements, the literature of the eighties has focused mainly on the assumption of transitivity and on the separability condition, the latter being responsible for the fact that in expected utility preferences are *linear* in the probabilities.

The so-called "preference reversal" phenomenon reported firstly by Lichtenstein and Slovic [1971], [1973] and confirmed by Grether and Plott [1979] is usually interpreted as a strong evidence against transitivity of preferences and has led to the development of non-transitive models of choice under risk and uncertainty. These include Fishburn's *skew symmetric bilinear (SSB) theory* [Fishburn 1982, 1984a] and its weakening, the *non-transitive convex utility theory* [Fishburn 1982], in the case of pure risk and the *regret theories* of Bell [1982], Loomes and Sugden [1982], [1987] as well as the general SSB model and its extensions [Fishburn 1984b, 1986a], [Fishburn and LaValle 1987] in the case of uncertainty.

However, as KARNI and SAFRA [1987] have shown the preference reversal phenomenon can also be interpreted as an additional evidence against the separability condition rather than as an evidence against transitivity of preferences (see also [HOLT 1986]).

Here, we are not concerned with the problems arising from the assumption of transitivity but with the evidence against the independence axiom. Thus, preferences are throughout assumed to be transitive.

There are two discernible approaches among the axiomatic models of transitive utility theory under risk relaxing the independence axiom. One maintains the *betweenness property* of expected utility theory, i.e. a probability mixture of two distributions is intermediate in preference between the individual distributions. Such a model was firstly axiomatized by CHEW [1983] and is known as the *weighted linear utility model.* We will discuss the weighted linear utility model and its extensions in sections 1.4.1 and 1.4.2.

The other approach – the one we are mainly concerned with here – can be labelled *rank-dependent utility theory.* This approach to the theory of choice under risk has its origin in Quiggin's *anticipated utility theory.* The anticipated utility model in turn can be best understood as a reaction to earlier theories of choice under risk including [EDWARDS 1955, 1962], [HANDA 1977], [KARMARKAR 1978], [KAHNEMAN AND TVERSKY 1979] which were motivated primarily from a descriptive point of view. The models proposed by those authors share the property that observed violations of expected utility maximizing behavior are explained by the hypothesis that a decision maker subjectively *distorts* given probabilities. The common structure of these proposals can be formally explained as follows.

Suppose that an individual has to choose among a given set of *lotteries* each lottery promising different monetary outcomes with some probability. According to expected utility theory there exists a function u defined on the set of outcomes such that the individual will choose the lottery F for which the value $V(F)$ given by

$$V(F) = \sum_{i=1}^{n} u(x_i)p_i \tag{1.1}$$

is maximal, where x_i are the outcomes of F and p_i are the corresponding probabilities with $\sum_1^n p_i = 1$. As this decision rule is known to be descriptively not valid[3] the suggestion was to extend the expected utility model by introducing a function $f : [0,1] \to \mathbf{R}$ such that the value of F is given by

$$V(F) = \sum_{i=1}^{n} u(x_i)f(p_i). \tag{1.2}$$

The corresponding decision rule would be to choose the lottery F for which the expression (1.2) is maximal.

To grasp the main problem with this suggestion it is convenient to introduce the notion of *first-order stochastic dominance.* A lottery F is said to dominate a lottery G by first-order stochastic dominance if for every possible outcome x the probability of winning more than x is always greater if F is played out than if G is played out. The principle of first-order stochastic dominance asserts that a decision maker should always prefer a lottery F to a lottery which is stochasically dominated by F. It seems to be clear that this principle is a very fundamental guide line for decision making under risk and it is hard to imagine an individual which would not want to behave in accordance with it. But it was realized by several authors (see e.g. [FISHBURN 1978], [QUIGGIN 1982] or [KARNI AND SCHMEIDLER 1990, section 3.4]) that unless the distortion function f is the identity the decision rule derived from (1.2) implies violations of the first-order stochastic dominance principle. However, in the case that f is the identity the functional (1.2) reduces to the functional (1.1). Thus, adding the

[3]see section 1.3.

requirement of consistency with the first-order stochastic dominance principle reduces the aforementioned proposals to the expected utility model.

To overcome this difficulty while retaining the idea of distorted probabilities QUIGGIN [1982] introduced in his model a function $h : [0,1] \to [0,1]$ which does not transform individual probabilities as in (1.2) but distorts in a certain manner the derived *cumulative probabilities.* More precisely, according to anticipated utility theory the value of a lottery F promising x_i with probability p_i is given by

$$V(F) = u(x_1)h(p_1) + \sum_{i=2}^{n} u(x_i) \left(h(\sum_{j=1}^{i} p_j) - h(\sum_{j=1}^{i-1} p_j) \right), \tag{1.3}$$

where it is assumed that $x_1 \leq ... \leq x_n$. The interpretation of equation (1.3) is that a decision maker takes into account not the probability of winning exactly the amount x_i but the probability of winning an amount *less or equal to* x_i. Then the corresponding utilities are cumulated while distorting these probabilities. It can be shown that the decision rule derived from (1.3) is in accordance with the principle of first-order stochastic dominance if the functions u and h are both strictly increasing. In section 1.4.3 the anticipated utility model will be considered again in more detail.

Building upon the idea of distortions of cumulative probabilities YAARI [1987], GREEN and JULLIEN [1988] and SEGAL [1989] developed variations and extensions of the anticipated utility approach. These will be treated in sections 1.4.4 and 1.4.5. Because of the functional form of equation (1.3) which requires the outcomes to be ranked in ascending order, the approach to decision making under risk initiated by Quiggin is referred to as the rank-dependent utility (RDU) approach.

1.2 The Axiomatic Basis of Expected Utility Theory

Let $X = [0, M] \subset \mathbf{R}$ denote a compact interval where $M > 0$. Throughout it will be assumed that the possible outcomes of a choice situation are the elements of the set X. Thus, the set X will also be referred to as the set of *prizes.* Prizes can be thought of as non-negative amounts of money up to the bound M which is the highest prize available. Note that the prize zero or the "status quo" is always included in the outcome set whereas losses are excluded.

The presence of *risk* is modelled through the set $D(X)$ of *cumulative distribution functions* on X. Formally, this set consists of all right-continuous, non-decreasing functions $F : X \to \mathbf{R}$ such that $F(0) \geq 0$ and $F(M) = 1$. Every function $F \in D(X)$ determines a unique probability measure P on X by the equation

$$P([0, x]) = F(x) \quad \text{for all } x \in X. \tag{1.4}$$

Conversely, to any probability measure on X there corresponds a unique element of $D(X)$ by means of equation (1.4) (see e.g. [BAUER 1968, p.123] for the details).

Thus, if an individual faces a risk represented by the cumulative distribution function F the number $F(x)$ is interpreted as the probability of receiving an amount less or equal to x.

Special attention is sometimes paid to the elements of $D(X)$ with finite range. These correspond to the probability measures with finite support and are denoted by $D^0(X)$. If F has finite range then F has also a finite set of discontinuity points $\{x_1, ..., x_n\}$. Denoting by p_i the "jump" of F at x_i then obviously $\sum_1^n p_i = 1$ and F corresponds to the probability distribution giving x_i with probability p_i for $i = 1, ..., n$. Such distributions are also referred to as *lotteries* or *prospects.* We will not distinguish between lotteries and their corresponding cumulative distribution functions and denote both by the vector $(x_1; p_1, ..., x_n; p_n)$ where in this notation it is always assumed that the outcomes are arranged in ascending order, i.e. $x_1 \leq ... \leq x_n$.

It is assumed that a decision maker has *preferences* among the elements of $D(X)$ described by a binary relation $\succeq$ on $D(X)$.

As usual, $\sim$ and $\succ$ denote the symmetric and asymmetric part of $\succeq$, respectively. The relation $\succeq$ is said to be *complete* if for all $F, G \in D(X)$, $F \succeq G$ or $G \succeq F$ holds. The relation $\succeq$ is said to be *transitive* if $F \succeq G$ and $G \succeq H$ imply $F \succeq H$ for all $F, G, H \in D(X)$. Finally, a relation $\succeq$ is called a *weak order* or a *preference relation* if $\succeq$ is complete and transitive.

A real-valued functional $V : D(X) \to \mathbf{R}$ is a *representation* of $\succeq$ if for all $F, G \in D(X)$

$$F \succeq G \Leftrightarrow V(F) \geq V(G).$$

Obviously, if such a representation exists the relation $\succeq$ is a weak order. Since we will only deal with preferences which admit such a representation, we will assume throughout the following axiom to be satisfied.

Axiom 1 (Weak Order) *The relation $\succeq$ is a weak order, i.e. preferences are complete and transitive.*

There are several possibilities to ensure the existence of a real-valued representation $V : D(X) \to \mathbf{R}$ for the preference relation $\succeq$. Essentially, preferences must satisfy some kind of *continuity* condition. Here, a quite strong form of continuity will be adopted to guarantee the existence of integral representations for all the theories considered in the sequel.

A sequence $(F_n)_{n=1}^{\infty}$ of cumulative distribution functions on X is said to *converge weakly* to $F \in D(X)$ if $F_n(x) \to F(x)$ at every continuity point x of F. The topology on $D(X)$ corresponding to this notion of convergence is called the *topology of weak convergence*. From now on we will always assume $D(X)$ to be endowed with this topology. The continuity axiom applied here takes the following form.

Axiom 2 (Continuity) *For every $F \in D(X)$ the sets $\{G \in D(X) : G \succeq F\}$ and $\{G \in D(X) : F \succeq G\}$ are closed in the topology of weak convergence.*

It is well-known that axioms 1 and 2 are necessary and sufficient for the existence of a continuous real-valued representation $V : D(X) \to \mathbf{R}$ of the relation $\succeq$. The following theorem is proved in [DEBREU 1964].

Theorem 1.2.1 (Debreu) *Let $\succeq$ be a binary relation on $D(X)$. There exists a representation $V : D(X) \to \mathbf{R}$ of $\succeq$, continuous in the topology of weak convergence, if and only if $\succeq$ satisfies axioms 1 and 2, i.e. if and only if $\succeq$ is a continuous weak order.*

The *expected utility model* requires the representation of theorem 1.2.1 to have the special form

$$V(F) = \int_0^M u(x)dF(x) \quad \text{for all } F \in D(X), \tag{1.5}$$

which is the mathematical expectation of the function $u : X \to \mathbf{R}$ with respect to the distribution F. If $F \in D^0(X)$ corresponds to the lottery $(x_1; p_1, ..., x_n; p_n)$ the functional (1.5) reduces to

$$V(F) = \sum_{i=1}^{n} u(x_i)p_i. \tag{1.6}$$

The additional condition on the preference relation implying the existence of such a representation is the well-known *independence axiom.*

Axiom 3 (Independence) *For all $F, G, H \in D(X)$ and all $\alpha \in [0, 1]$, $F \succeq G$ implies $\alpha F + (1 - \alpha)H \succeq \alpha G + (1 - \alpha)H$.*

Before the expected utility theorem is formally stated some remarks on the independence axiom are in order.

Firstly, observe that in our notation $\alpha F + (1 - \alpha)H$ refers unambigously to the cumulative distribution function defined pointwise by

$$(\alpha F + (1 - \alpha)H)(x) = \alpha F(x) + (1 - \alpha)H(x),$$

for $x \in X$.

However, if F and H are interpreted as (finite) lotteries the term $\alpha F + (1 - \alpha)H$ has two different meanings. The first interpretation views this term as the *one-stage* lottery giving the outcomes occuring in F and H with the corresponding probabilities multiplied by α and $1 - \alpha$, respectively. In this interpretation the term $\alpha F + (1 - \alpha)H$ is referred to as the *probability mixture* of F and H. It is this meaning which is usually employed in calculations and which is always intended here.

On the other hand, the normative appeal of the independence axiom is often explained by interpreting the term $\alpha F + (1 - \alpha)H$ as the *two-stage* lottery giving the *lotteries* F and H with probability α and $1 - \alpha$, respectively. Under this interpretation the independence axiom asserts that if there is a preference for F over G there should also be a preference for the α-chance of participating in the lottery F over the α-chance of participating in the lottery G if otherwise in both cases the lottery H is played out.

It should be emphasized that the two interpretations are equivalent only under additional assumptions about how two-stage lotteries are to be transformed into one-stage lotteries. The standard assumption in this context is the *reduction axiom* which implies that a decision maker is indifferent between the two-stage lottery $\alpha F + (1 - \alpha)H$ and the corresponding probability mixture. Thus, the reduction axiom justifies the use of the two-stage argument for the independence axiom as it is stated here. However, the reduction axiom is far from being uncontroversial and there are recent attempts to explain the bad performance of the expected utility model by violations of the reduction axiom.[4]

The expected utility theorem was firstly proved in [v.NEUMANN AND MORGENSTERN 1947]. Later, HERSTEIN and MILNOR [1953] simplified the original proof. A proof of the version stated here can be found in [GRANDMONT 1972].

Theorem 1.2.2 (The Expected Utility Theorem) *Let $\succeq$ be a binary relation on $D(X)$. There exists a continuous function $u : X \to \mathbf{R}$ such that the functional (1.5) represents $\succeq$ if and only if $\succeq$ satisfies axioms 1,2 and 3. Moreover, the function u is unique up to positive affine transformations, i.e. if $u^* : X \to \mathbf{R}$ is a function such that $F \mapsto \int_X u^*(x)dF(x)$ represents $\succeq$ then there exist real numbers $a > 0$ and b with $u^*(x) = au(x) + b$ for all $x \in X$.*

The function u is called the *v.Neumann-Morgenstern utility function.* It is worth noting that the independence axiom gives a *cardinal* utility function defined on the set of outcomes derived from *ordinal* preferences among distributions.

Observe also that the continuity axiom 2 is strong enough to imply the continuity of the v.Neumann-Morgenstern utility function.

Besides continuity another natural requirement is that the v.Neumann-Morgenstern utility should be an increasing function of the variable x. Indeed, this property of the function u follows from the principle of first-order stochastic dominance which is held to be a fundamental principle of rational decision-making under risk.

[4] For an analysis of decision making under risk without the reduction axiom and in particular a new foundation of expected utility theory without this axiom see [Segal 1990].

A distribution F is said to dominate a distribution G by *first-order stochastic dominance* if $F(x) \leq G(x)$ for all $x \in X$ with strict inequality for at least one $x \in X$.

The following axiom – also known as the principle of first-order stochastic dominance – requires preferences to be *monotone* with respect to first-order stochastic dominance. Note that monotonicity is intended in the strict sense.

Axiom 4 (Monotonicity) *For all $F, G \in D(X)$, $F \succ G$ whenever F dominates G by first-order stochastic dominance.*

Let δ_x denote the *degenerate* lottery giving $x \in X$ with probability 1. Obviously, δ_x dominates δ_y by first-order stochastic dominance if and only if $x > y$. Since for the expected utility functional V in (1.6) one has $u(x) = V(\delta_x)$, axiom 4 implies that u is strictly increasing.

Conversely, a simple argument using the continuity of the v.Neumann-Morgenstern utility shows that if u is strictly increasing preferences are (strictly) monotone with respect to first-order stochastic dominance. Thus, in expected utility theory axiom 4 is equivalent to u being strictly increasing.

A somewhat stronger result concerning the connection between expected utility maximizing behavior and the notion of first-order stochastic dominance is provided by the following theorem due to HADAR and RUSSELL [1969].

Theorem 1.2.3 (Hadar and Russell) *Let $F, G \in D(X)$; then F first-order stochastically dominates G if and only if*

$$\int_0^M u(x)dF(x) > \int_0^M u(x)dG(x)$$

for every continuous, strictly increasing function $u : X \to \mathbf{R}$.

1.3 The Empirical Evidence against the Independence Axiom

The main feature of the expected utility model is that the derived representation of preferences is *linear in the probabilities*. As the expected utility theorem of the previous section shows the condition responsible for this fact is the independence axiom. However, there is now a broad agreement among psychologists and economists that probabilities are not treated by decision makers in such a simple way.

One of the earliest examples of systematic violation of linearity in the probabilities – or equivalently, of the independence axiom – is the well-known *Allais paradox* [ALLAIS 1953, 1979]. The famous example involves preference comparisons within the following two pairs of lotteries (1 m. = 1 million).

$$a_1 : \{1.00 \text{ chance of \$ 1 m. versus } a_2 : \begin{cases} 0.10 \text{ chance of \$ 5 m.} \\ 0.89 \text{ chance of \$ 1 m.} \\ 0.01 \text{ chance of \$ 0} \end{cases}$$

and

$$a_3 : \begin{cases} 0.11 \text{ chance of \$ 1 m.} \\ 0.89 \text{ chance of \$ 0} \end{cases} \quad \text{versus } a_4 : \begin{cases} 0.10 \text{ chance of \$ 5 m.} \\ 0.90 \text{ chance of \$ 0} \end{cases}$$

Under the expected utility hypothesis a preference for a_1 over a_2 in the first pair implies a preference for a_3 over a_4 in the second pair. This can easily be seen as follows. Assuming without loss of generality $u(0) = 0$, the preference $a_1 \succ a_2$ implies

$$u(1000000) > 0.1u(5000000) + 0.89u(1000000),$$

thus

$$0.11u(1000000) > 0.1u(5000000),$$

and therefore $a_3 \succ a_4$. But researchers such as ALLAIS [1953] or SLOVIC and TVERSKY [1974] have found that the majority preferences of subjects is for a_1 in the first pair and for a_4 in the second, thus violating the independence axiom.

There are two possible replies to the phenomenon described by the Allais paradox. One criticism of this evidence has been that individuals whose choices violated the independence axiom would correct themselves once the structure of the example has been elucidated by the above computation. It is this attitude which had been taken for instance by Savage who – as a defender of the expected utility hypothesis – also chose a_1 and a_4 when firstly presented with this example. But in subsequent empirical investigations it turned out that the observed choices remained persistent even after theoretical explanations about the implications of the expected utility hypothesis.

Another criticism has been that the Allais paradox is an isolated example whose persuasive power depends on the special data of the involved lotteries. Again, it turned out that this argument is wrong and the Allais paradox is now known to be just a special case of a general empirical pattern termed the *common consequence effect.* This effect involves the following two pairs of lotteries.

$$b_1 : \alpha\delta_x + (1-\alpha)P^{**} \text{ versus } b_2 : \alpha P + (1-\alpha)P^{**}$$

and

$$b_3 . \alpha\delta_x + (1-\alpha)P^{*} \text{ versus } b_4 : \alpha P + (1-\alpha)P^{*},$$

where P is a lottery with outcomes both greater and less x, and P^{**} stochastically dominates P^*.

In empirical studies it was confirmed that a majority of subjects exhibit a preference for b_1 in the first pair and for b_4 in the second pair. Obviously, because of the "common consequence" P^{**} in the first pair and P^* in the second pair this choice contradicts the independence axiom.

The original Allais paradox corresponds to $\alpha = 0.11$, $x = 1000000$, the lotteries $P^* = \delta_0, P^{**} = \delta_{1000000}$ and P giving 0 with probability

1/11 and 5000000 with probability 10/11.[5]

A second class of systematic violations of the independence axiom, stemming from another early example of ALLAIS [1953], is known as the *common ratio effect.* Consider the following pairs of lotteries.

$$c_1 = (0; 1-p, x; p) \text{ versus } c_2 = (0; 1-q, y; q)$$

and

$$c_3 = (0; 1-rp, x; rp) \text{ versus } c_4 = (0; 1-rq, y; rq),$$

where $0 < q < p$, $0 < x < y$ and $r \in (0,1)$.

Since $c_{i+2} = rc_i + (1-r)\delta_0$ for $i = 1, 2$ a preference $c_1 \succ c_2$ implies by the independence axiom $c_3 \succ c_4$. Empirical studies, however, have shown that there is a tendency of subjects to depart from this prediction and choose c_1 in the first pair and c_4 in the second. The name of this phenomenon comes from the common factor r in the lotteries c_3 and c_4.

A concrete example of this pattern has been tested by KAHNEMAN and TVERSKY [1979]. They found that with $x = 3000$ (Israeli pounds), $y = 4000$, $p = 1$, $q = 0.8$ and $r = 0.25$ as the values for the parameters, 80 percent of their subjects preferred c_1 in the first pair and 65 percent preferred c_4 in the second pair. Because of the certainty in c_1 this form of the common ratio effect is also known as the *certainty effect.*

The common ratio effect plays an important role in our analysis of choice under risk and will be considered again in chapter 2.

Summarizing, the lesson which should be drawn from the above examples is that, in contrary to what the independence axiom claims, the utility evaluation of outcomes in a lottery may well depend on the

[5]For a further discussion of the common consequence effect and similar generalizations of the Allais paradox see [Machina 1987], [Segal 1987a], [Green and Jullien 1988].

unrealized alternatives. As BELL [1985, p.1] has put it, "winning the top prize of $10,000 in a lottery may leave one much happier than receiving $10,000 as the lowest prize in a lottery."

For a further discussion of the empirical evidence concerning choice under risk and uncertainty the reader is referred to the survey article by MACHINA [1987] from which this exposition has benefitted a lot.

1.4 Non-Linear Utility Theory under Risk

In this section the most important alternative theories of transitive choice under risk which do not assume the full strength of the independence axiom but different weakenings are presented.[6] A common characteristic of these models is the attempt to accommodate the behavioral patterns described in the previous section while retaining some of the normative appeal of the expected utility hypothesis. All theories discussed here satisfy the order and continuity axioms of section 1.2 and are consistent with the principle of first-order stochastic dominance (axiom 4).

1.4.1 Weighted Linear Utility Theory

The *weighted linear utility model* departs from the expected utility model by introducing a *weight function* $w : X \to \mathbf{R}$ such that a

[6]The Machina theory [Machina 1982] is not included here since it plays a special role in the theory of choice under risk. The approach taken by Machina can not be viewed as *one* model of choice under risk relaxing the independence axiom but rather as a general method of analyzing non-linear utility theory under risk. A version of this method will be used in chapter 3.

representation of preferences among distribution functions is given by

$$V(F) = \frac{\int_0^M u(x)w(x)dF(x)}{\int_0^M w(x)dF(x)} \quad \text{for all } F \in D(X). \tag{1.7}$$

It has been shown by CHEW [1983] that the representation (1.7) corresponds to the following weakening of the independence axiom known as the *weak substitution axiom.*

Axiom 5 (Weak Substitution) *For all $F, G \in D(X)$ and all $\alpha \in (0,1)$, $F \sim G$ implies the existence of $\beta \in (0,1)$ such that for all $H \in D(X)$, $\alpha F + (1-\alpha)H \sim \beta G + (1-\beta)H$.*

Clearly, this axiom is implied by the independence axiom which requires $\beta = \alpha$. The fact that in weighted linear utility theory the number β may differ from α leads to a substantial relaxation of the expected utility hypothesis. Note that the representation (1.7) reduces to the expected utility representation (1.5) if and only if the weight function w is constant.

In the case that F corresponds to $(x_1; p_1, ..., x_n; p_n)$ the functional in (1.7) reduces to

$$V(F) = \frac{\sum_{i=1}^n u(x_i)w(x_i)p_i}{\sum_{i=1}^n w(x_i)p_i}. \tag{1.8}$$

The representation theorem for weighted linear utility theory is proved in [CHEW 1983].

Theorem 1.4.1 (Chew) *Let $\succeq$ be a binary relation on $D(X)$. There exist continuous functions $u, w : X \to \mathbf{R}$, $w > 0$ such that the functional (1.7) represents $\succeq$ if and only if $\succeq$ satisfies axioms 1,2 and 5.*

The uniqueness properties of the functions u, w and the conditions under which the functional V in (1.7) satisfies axiom 4 (monotonicity with respect to first-order stochastic dominance) are also given in [CHEW 1983] to which the reader is referred. A different axiomatization of the weighted linear utility model has been obtained by FISHBURN [1983].

There are two possible interpretations of the weighted linear utility representation (see also [KARNI AND SCHMEIDLER 1990]). Firstly, one may define for each lottery $F = (x_1; p_1, ..., x_n; p_n)$ a corresponding lottery $F^w \in D^0(X)$ by $F^w = (x_1; p_1^w, ..., x_n; p_n^w)$ where

$$p_i^w = \frac{w(x_i)p_i}{\sum_{i=1}^n w(x_i)p_i} \qquad \text{for } i = 1, ..., n. \tag{1.9}$$

Then the representation (1.8) of $\succeq$ on $D^0(X)$ can be rewritten as

$$V(F) = \sum_{i=1}^n u(x_i)p_i^w,$$

which is the expected utility of the distribution F^w.

Thus, one interpretation of weighted linear utility is in terms of a *distortion* of probabilities, the distortion being given by (1.9). For example, if w is a decreasing function of x then the resulting distortion implies overestimation of the probabilities corresponding to small prizes and underestimation of the probabilities corresponding to high prizes. The resulting representation therefore captures a *pessimistic* attitude towards risk.

On the other hand, one may also define a modified utility function $u^w : X \to \mathbf{R}$ by

$$u^w(x_i) = \frac{u(x_i)w(x_i)}{\sum_{i=1}^n w(x_i)p_i} \qquad \text{for } i = 1, ..., n.$$

Then (1.8) can be rewritten as

$$V(F) = \sum_{i=1}^n u^w(x_i)p_i,$$

which is the expected utility of the modified utility function u^w with respect to the distribution F. Observe that the modified utility function depends not only on u but also on the distribution F.

For the verification that the weighted linear utility model is consistent with the evidence raised by the Allais paradox and the common ratio effect if the weight function is suitably specified see e.g. [CHEW 1983] or [CHEW AND WALLER 1986].

1.4.2 Theories with the Betweenness Property

The weighted linear utility model turned out to be just a special case of a more general class of theories. The models belonging to this class share the so-called *betweenness property* which asserts that a probability mixture of two distributions is intermediate in preference between the individual distributions. Formally, the betweenness property can be stated as follows.

Property 6 (Betweenness) *For all* $F, G \in D(X)$ *and all* $\alpha \in (0,1)$, $F \succ G$ *implies* $F \succ \alpha F + (1-\alpha)G \succ G$.

Note that betweenness implies that preferences are both quasiconvex and quasiconcave.

Axiomatizations of preference models satisfying betweenness were independently developed by CHEW [1985], DEKEL [1986] and FISHBURN [1986b].

The essential condition in the context of betweenness conforming utility theory is the following weakening of axiom 5, known as the *very weak substitution axiom.*

Axiom 7 (Very Weak Substitution) *For all* $F, G, H \in D(X)$ *and* $\alpha \in (0,1)$, $F \sim G$ *implies the existence of* $\beta \in (0,1)$ *such that* $\alpha F + (1-\alpha)H \sim \beta G + (1-\beta)H$.

In contrast to weak substitution, axiom 7 allows the number β to depend also on the distribution H. The following theorem is proved in [CHEW 1989a] where it is also shown that axioms 2 and 7 together imply betweenness.

Theorem 1.4.2 (Chew) *Let $\succeq$ be a binary relation on $D(X)$. There exists a function $\phi : X \times X \to \mathbf{R}$ with $\phi(\cdot, y)$ continuous for each $y \in X$ and $\phi(x,x) = 0$ for all $x \in X$ such that a representation $V : D(X) \to \mathbf{R}$ of $\succeq$ is given by the unique solution $V(F) = y$ of*

$$\int_0^M \phi(x,y)dF(x) = 0 \quad \textit{for all } F \in D(X), \tag{1.10}$$

if and only if $\succeq$ satisfies axioms 1,2 and 7.

The representation obtained in the theorem is referred to as the *implicit weighted utility representation.* The idea underlying the functional form of this representation is best understood in terms of the certainty equivalent of a distribution. The *certainty equivalent* $C(F)$ of a distribution F is defined as the sure gain to which the distribution F is indifferent. Formally, $C(F)$ is implicitly given as the solution to

$$\delta_{C(F)} \sim F. \tag{1.11}$$

Under monotonicity of preferences the number $C(F)$ always exists and is uniquely determined by (1.11). Furthermore, if $V : D(X) \to \mathbf{R}$ is a representation of preferences then $C : D(X) \to \mathbf{R}$ defined by $V(\delta_{C(F)}) = V(F)$ represents the same preference relation. Thus, equation (1.10) determines directly the certainty equivalent representation of the preference relation $\succeq$ on $D(X)$.

For example, the weighted linear certainty equivalent corresponds to $\phi(x,y) = w(x)(u(x) - u(y))$ in which case equation (1.10) admits an explicit solution.

For a further analysis of implicit weighted utility theory and a survey of axiomatic utility theories with the betweenness property see [Chew 1989a].

1.4.3 Anticipated Utility Theory

The *anticipated utility representation* of $F = (x_1; p_1, ..., x_n; p_n)$ takes the following form (see also section 1.1).

$$V(F) = u(x_1)h(p_1) + \sum_{i=2}^{n} u(x_i) \left(h(\sum_{j=1}^{i} p_j) - h(\sum_{j=1}^{i-1} p_j) \right), \qquad (1.12)$$

where $u : X \to \mathbf{R}$ is a utility function and $h : [0,1] \to [0,1]$ is a strictly increasing, surjective *transformation function.* We recall that in our notation the outcomes x_i are assumed to be arranged in ascending order, which is essential for the representation (1.12). Therefore, anticipated utility theory is also known as the theory of *expected utility with rank-dependent probabilities.* Clearly, the expected utility model corresponds to the case where h is the identity function.

The first axiomatization of the anticipated utility model is due to QUIGGIN [1982]. Among his axioms, imposed on a preference relation $\succeq$ on the set $D^0(X)$, the essential condition implying the existence of the representation (1.12) is the following so-called *weak certainty equivalent substitution axiom.*

Axiom 8 (Weak Certainty Equivalent Substitution) *For all F and G in $D^0(X)$, if $F = (x_1; p_1, ..., x_n; p_n)$ and $G = (y_1; p_1, ..., y_n; p_n)$ then*

$$\frac{1}{2}\delta_{C(F)} + \frac{1}{2}\delta_{C(G)} \sim (c_1; p_1, ..., c_n; p_n), \qquad (1.13)$$

where $c_i = C(\frac{1}{2}\delta_{x_i} + \frac{1}{2}\delta_{y_i})$.

The interpretation of axiom 8 is as follows. There are two ways of reducing the two-stage lottery offering the lotteries F and G with probability 1/2. The first reduces the two-stage lottery to the one-stage lottery at the left hand side of (1.13) where F and G are replaced by their certainty equivalents. The second involves changing the order of summation and then replacing each of the lotteries $\frac{1}{2}\delta_{x_i} + \frac{1}{2}\delta_{y_i}$ by their certainty equivalent to obtain the right hand side of (1.13).

It is not difficult to show that axiom 8 is implied by the independence axiom. This can be seen for instance by observing that in expected utility theory the reduced lotteries in (1.13) are both equivalent to the lottery giving each of the outcomes x_i and y_i with probability $p_i/2$ for $i = 1, ..., n$.

An important consequence of axiom 8 is that the transformation function h satisfies $h(1/2) = 1/2$. This property, however, turned out to be undesirable because it prevents the representation V to display risk aversion (see chapter 3). On the other hand, SEGAL [1989] and CHEW [1989b] have shown that this property is not essential for the anticipated utility model and provided alternative axiomatizations without this restriction. The set of axioms proposed by Segal will be discussed in section 1.4.5.

The extension of the representation (1.12) to $D(X)$ is given by

$$V(F) = \int_0^M u(x)d(h \circ F)(x) \quad \text{for all } F \in D(X), \tag{1.14}$$

which is the expectation of u with respect to the transformed distribution $h \circ F$.

It will be convenient to work in the sequel not only with the transformation function h but also with the function $f : [0,1] \to [0,1]$ defined by the equation $f(p) = 1 - h(1-p)$. Note that $h(0) = 0$, $h(1) = 1$ and $h(1/2) = 1/2$ imply $f(1) = 1$, $f(0) = 0$ and $f(1/2) = 1/2$, respectively. Also, f is strictly increasing and surjective if and only if h is. With the use of the function f instead of h equation (1.14) reads

$$V(F) = -\int_0^M u(x)df(1 - F(x)) \quad \text{for all } F \in D(X), \tag{1.15}$$

and (1.12) can be rewritten as

$$V(F) = u(x_1) + \sum_{i=2}^{n}(u(x_i) - u(x_{i-1}))f(\sum_{j=i}^{n} p_j) \tag{1.16}$$

if F corresponds to the lottery $(x_1; p_1, ..., x_n; p_n)$.

An analysis of the Allais paradox and the common ratio effect within the framework of anticipated utility theory can be found in [SEGAL 1987a]. Consider for instance the lotteries c_i of the common ratio effect discussed in section 1.3. Assuming without loss of generality $u(0) = 0$, equation (1.16) implies $V(c_1) = u(x)f(p)$, $V(c_2) = u(y)f(q)$, $V(c_3) = u(x)f(rp)$ and $V(c_4) = u(y)f(rq)$, respectively. It has been shown in [SEGAL 1987a] that a possible explanation for the choice of c_1 in the first pair and of c_4 in the second pair of the common ratio effect is that the *elasticity* of f is strictly increasing. Indeed, if the elasticity of f at p, defined by $pf'(p)/f(p)$, is strictly increasing it follows that the function $f(rp)/f(rq)$ is strictly increasing in r. Thus, it may happen that

$$\frac{f(rp)}{f(rq)} < \frac{u(y)}{u(x)} < \frac{f(p)}{f(q)},$$

which implies the behavior exhibited by the common ratio effect.

Similar considerations show that the behavior exhibited by the Allais paradox can be explained by specific assumptions about the shape of the transformation function f (see [SEGAL 1987a]).

1.4.4 The Dual Theory

A special case of the anticipated utility model has been axiomatized by YAARI [1987]. The so-called *dual theory* emerges by interchanging the roles of payments and probabilities in the expected utility model. Thus, in the dual theory the representation is *linear in the payments* but not necessarily linear in the probabilities.

The dual representation of preferences is given by

$$V(F) = \int_0^M x d(h \circ F)(x) \quad \text{for all } F \in D(X), \tag{1.17}$$

where the linearity in the payments corresponds to the linearity of the utility function. Obviously, this representation is a special case of (1.14). Nevertheless the dual theory deserves interest on their own rights because of a surprisingly simple set of axioms implying the existence of the representation (1.17).

To state the essential axiom it is convenient to introduce the following notation. Let Z and Y denote the random variables underlying the distribution functions F and G, respectively. For every $\alpha \in [0,1]$, the expression $\alpha F \oplus (1-\alpha)G$ refers to the cumulative distribution function corresponding to the random variable $\alpha Z + (1-\alpha)Y$. The following axiom is known as the *dual independence axiom*.

Axiom 9 (Dual Independence) *For all $F, G, H \in D(X)$ and all $\alpha \in [0,1]$, $F \succeq G$ implies $\alpha F \oplus (1-\alpha)H \succeq \alpha G \oplus (1-\alpha)H$.*

The representation theorem for the dual theory is proved in [YAARI 1987].

Theorem 1.4.3 (Yaari) *Let $\succeq$ be a binary relation on $D(X)$. There exists a continuous, strictly increasing and surjective function $h : [0,1] \to [0,1]$ such that (1.17) represents $\succeq$ if and only if $\succeq$ satisfies axioms 1,2,4 and 9.*

Like the more general model of anticipated utility the dual theory is consistent with the empirical patterns described in section 1.3. But as the dual theory just interchanges the roles payments and probabilities play in expected utility theory it is easy to construct "dual" paradoxes within Yaari's model.

There is, however, a second feature of the dual theory which deserves interest. In expected utility theory it is known that the notion of *risk aversion* is equivalent to concavity of the v.Neumann-Morgenstern utility function. Thus, in expected utility theory risk aversion is also equivalent to *diminishing marginal utility of wealth.* But as YAARI [1987, p.95] has pointed out, the notions of risk aversion and marginal utility of wealth are at a very fundamental level distinct concepts. One important intention of the dual theory is to show that these concepts can be separated from each other. Indeed, the dual theory allows for risk aversion although there is clearly no diminishing marginal utility of wealth since $u(x) = x$ for $x \in X$. The issue concerning risk aversion and diminishing marginal utility of wealth will be discussed in more detail in chapter 3.

1.4.5 The General Rank-Dependent Utility Model

The anticipated utility model, and hence also the dual theory, turned out to be just a special case of a more general model of transitive preferences over probability distributions. This has been observed independently by GREEN and JULLIEN [1988] and SEGAL [1989].[7] The essential condition distinguishing the *rank-dependent utility (RDU) model* from other theories is the following axiom which is called *ordinal independence axiom* in [GREEN AND JULLIEN 1988] and – in a slightly different version – *irrelevance axiom* in [SEGAL 1989].

Axiom 10 (Ordinal Independence) *For all $F, F', G, G' \in D(X)$ and all $x \in X$, if $F = F'$, $G = G'$ on $[0, x)$ (resp. on $[x, M]$) and $F = G$, $F' = G'$ on $[x, M]$ (resp. on $[0, x)$) then $F \succeq G \Leftrightarrow F' \succeq G'$.*

The interpretation of the ordinal independence axiom is as follows. Suppose that the cumulative distribution functions F and G coincide above some point $x \in X$. Then the preference between F and G does not depend on how the common tail is shaped. The same holds if F and G coincide below the point $x \in X$.

Axiom 10 is implied by the independence axiom. It is not easy to prove this directly, but it follows immediately using the expected

[7] Apparently, the development of the general RDU model has its origin in [Segal 1984].

utility representation (1.5). The essential property of the representation (1.5) implying the ordinal independence axiom is that the integral can be splitted into an integral over $[0, x)$ and an integral over $[x, M]$. Axiom 10 follows then by substituting F' and G' for F and G, respectively.

The representation theorem for the RDU model is proved in the following form in the appendix of [GREEN AND JULLIEN 1988].

Theorem 1.4.4 (Green and Jullien) *Let $\succeq$ be a binary relation on the set $D(X)$. There exists a function $\psi : X \times [0,1] \to \mathbf{R}$, continuous in each argument, satisfying $\psi(\cdot, 0) = 0$ and*

$$\psi(y,q) - \psi(y,p) - \psi(x,q) + \psi(x,p) > 0 \quad \textit{for } y > x, q > p, \qquad (1.18)$$

such that

$$V(F) = \psi(x_1, 1) + \sum_{i=2}^{n} \left(\psi(x_i, \sum_{j=i}^{n} p_j) - \psi(x_{i-1}, \sum_{j=i}^{n} p_j) \right) \qquad (1.19)$$

represents $\succeq$ on $D^0(X)$ if and only if $\succeq$ satisfies axioms 1,2,4 and 10.

In the sequel, the functional V in (1.19) will be referred to as the *RDU functional* corresponding to the preference relation $\succeq$.

The anticipated utility model corresponds to the case where in theorem 1.4.4 the function ψ is multiplicatively separable in the variables x and p, i.e. $\psi(x,p) = u(x)f(p)$ for suitable functions $u : X \to \mathbf{R}$ and $f : [0,1] \to [0,1]$. Indeed, the representation (1.19) reduces in that case to (1.16) and the condition (1.18) asserts that u and f are both strictly increasing.

A somewhat different approach to the RDU model, and in particular to the ordinal independence principle, has been taken by SEGAL [1989]. He observed that the existence of the representation (1.19) is closely related to the existence of a measure μ on $X \times [0,1]$ such that a representation of preferences is given by the area of the epigraph of a distribution function with respect to the measure μ.

The *epigraph* e_F in $X \times [0,1]$ of a distribution function $F \in D(X)$ is defined as follows.

$$e_F = cl\{(x,p) \in X \times [0,1] : p \geq F(x)\} \quad \text{for } F \in D(X),$$

where $cl\,A$ denotes the closure of the set A.

Consider first the expected value of a distribution $F \in D(X)$ given by

$$E(F) = \int_0^M x dF(x).$$

The following integration-by-parts argument shows that $E(F)$ is the area of e_F with respect to the Lebesgue measure.

$$\begin{aligned}\int_0^M x dF(x) &= xF(x)|_0^M - \int_0^M F(x)dx \\ &= \int_0^M (1 - F(x))dx \\ &= \int_0^M \int_{F(x)}^1 dpdx.\end{aligned}$$

Similarily, the expected utility of F can be transformed to show that the expected utility representation equals the area of e_F with respect to a product measure where the measure of an interval $[x,y]$ on the prize axis is given by $u(y) - u(x)$ and the measure on the probability axis is again the Lebesgue measure.

The anticipated utility functional (1.14) corresponds to the case where the measure μ is a general product measure. Integrating by parts the anticipated utility of F and assuming $u(0) = 0$ yields

$$\begin{aligned}\int_0^M u(x)d(h \circ F)(x) &= u(x)(h \circ F)(x)|_0^M - \int_0^M (h \circ F)(x)du(x) \\ &= \int_0^M (1 - (h \circ F)(x))du(x) \\ &= \int_0^M \int_{F(x)}^1 dh(p)du(x).\end{aligned}$$

Obviously, the last expression is the area of e_F with respect to a product measure where the measure of an interval $[x, y]$ on the prize axis is given by $u(y) - u(x)$ and the measure of an interval $[p, q]$ on the probability axis is given by $h(q) - h(p)$.

The general RDU model corresponds to the case where the measure μ on $X \times [0,1]$ is not necessarily a product measure. The following theorem is proved in [SEGAL 1989].

Theorem 1.4.5 (Segal) *Let $\succeq$ be a binary relation on $D(X)$. There exists a continuous* [8] *measure μ on $X \times [0,1]$ with $\mu(A) > 0$ for every non-empty open set $A \subset X \times [0,1]$ such that*

$$F \succeq G \Leftrightarrow \mu(e_F) \geq \mu(e_G) \quad \textit{for all } F \in D(X), \tag{1.20}$$

if and only if $\succeq$ satisfies axioms 1,2,4 and 10.

In the sequel, a measure on $X \times [0,1]$ representing a preference relation $\succeq$ according to (1.20) will be called the *epigraph measure* corresponding to $\succeq$.

The connection between the theorem above and theorem 1.4.4 can be explained as follows. Suppose that $\psi : X \times [0,1] \to \mathbf{R}$ is a function satisfying the conditions of theorem 1.4.4. Define a measure μ on the set of all closed rectangles in $X \times [0,1]$ by

$$\mu([x,y] \times [1-q, 1-p]) = \psi(y,q) - \psi(y,p) - \psi(x,q) + \psi(x,p).$$

There exists a unique extension of this measure to all Borel sets of $X \times [0,1]$, which we also denote by μ. Since ψ is continuous in each argument μ has no pointmass. Therefore, by the properties of the Lebesgue extension μ is continuous in the sense of theorem 1.4.5. The fact that μ is positive on every non-empty open set follows immediately from (1.18) and it is easy to verify that for every $F \in D^0(X)$ one has

[8] Continuity means here that μ as well as the induced marginal measures are atomless, and μ satisfies $\mu(A_n) \to \mu(A)$ whenever $\limsup A_n = \liminf A_n = A$.

$\mu(e_F) = V(F) - \psi(0,1)$ if $V(F)$ is defined by equation (1.19). Thus, the measure μ defined in this way represents preferences in the sense of equation (1.20) on $D^0(X)$ and by continuous extension also on $D(X)$.

Let now conversely μ be a measure on $X \times [0,1]$ as given by theorem 1.4.5. Define a function $\psi : X \times [0,1] \to \mathbf{R}$ by

$$\psi(x,p) = \mu([0,x] \times [1-p,1]) \quad \text{for all } (x,p) \in X \times [0,1].$$

Since μ is continuous ψ is continuous in each argument. Since μ has positive value on every non-empty open subset of X the function ψ satisfies condition (1.18). Finally, the functional form of the representation (1.19) follows from additivity of the measure μ.

Summarizing, it is shown that theorems 1.4.4 and 1.4.5 are in fact equivalent in the sense that each one can be derived from the other.[9]

There have been several additional conditions suggested to ensure that the measure μ of theorem 1.4.5, or equivalently the function ψ in theorem 1.4.4, admits the form of a product, thus yielding the anticipated utility functional (without Quiggin's restriction $f(1/2) = 1/2$). SEGAL [1989] proposed an axiom which he called *projection independence.* However, unlike the ordinal independence axiom this axiom does not admit a clear behavioral interpretation. In section 2.5 another condition in terms of *relative utility* (see also 2.4) is suggested. An axiom imposed directly on the preference relation implying in connection with ordinal independence the anticipated utility representation has been recently obtained by CHATEAUNEUF [1990]. But also his axiom is of a quite complex structure and it is not very easy to grasp its behavioral implications.

Thus, the difficulty to characterize the anticipated utility model by plausible behavioral conditions seems to indicate that it is more na-

[9]The fact that theorem 1.4.4 gives the representation of preferences only on $D^0(X)$ does not really pose a problem since by continuity of preferences a representation on $D(X)$ is uniquely determined by its restriction to $D^0(X)$.

tural to consider the general RDU model characterized by the ordinal independence principle.

1.4.6 Implicit Rank-Linear Utility Theory

We conclude our review of non-expected utility theory with some remarks on a very general model of transitive preferences over probability distributions proposed recently by CHEW and EPSTEIN [1989]. This model, called *implicit rank-linear utility theory*, contains all models so far presented as special cases. Chew and Epstein observed that the implicit weighted utility approach as well as the RDU approach involve *separability conditions* in the outcome space. However, these conditions have a very different structure within the two approaches. To illustrate this fact it is proved below that the only utility model satisfying both, very weak substitution and ordinal independence, is the expected utility model. Implicit rank-linear utility theory can neither be viewed as a natural extension of implicit weighted utility theory nor as a natural extension of RDU theory. It is, however, surprising that such a general model as the implicit rank-linear utility model still implies the existence of a representation of a specific functional form. For the formulation of the representation theorem and the details concerning implicit rank-linear utility theory the reader is referred to [CHEW AND EPSTEIN 1989] and [WAKKER 1990b].

Lemma 1.4.6 *Let $\succeq$ be a binary relation on $D(X)$ satisfying axioms 1,2 and 4. If $\succeq$ satisfies in addition very weak substitution (axiom 7) and ordinal independence (axiom 10) then $\succeq$ satisfies the independence axiom (axiom 3), i.e. $\succeq$ admits an expected utility representation.*

Proof. Since the betweenness property implies that the indifference curves in the *Marschak-Machina triangle* (see the figure below) are straight lines it suffices to show that the expected utility functional is the only RDU functional with straight lines as indifference curves.

Consider for fixed outcomes $x_1 < x_2 < x_3$ the following set of lotteries:

$$L = \{(x_1; p_1, x_2; 1 - p_1 - p_3, x_3; p_3) : p_1, p_3 \in [0, 1], p_1 + p_3 \leq 1\}.$$

Let ψ be the function given by theorem 1.4.4 and $V : D(X) \to \mathbf{R}$ the corresponding representation of $\succeq$ according to (1.19). Without loss of generality it is assumed that ψ is differentiable with respect to the second argument. The derivative is denoted by ψ_2. The set of (p_1, p_3) for which $V|_L$ is constant can be locally parametrized by p_1. It is easily verified that the slope of these *indifference curves* is given by

$$\frac{dp_3}{dp_1} = \frac{\psi_2(x_2, 1 - p_1) - \psi_2(x_1, 1 - p_1)}{\psi_2(x_3, p_3) - \psi_2(x_2, p_3)}.$$

Since $\succeq$ is assumed to satisfy very weak substitution it satisfies also the betweenness property. Thus, preferences are both quasiconcave and quasiconvex on the set L which in turn implies that the indifference curves must be straight lines as shown in the following figure.

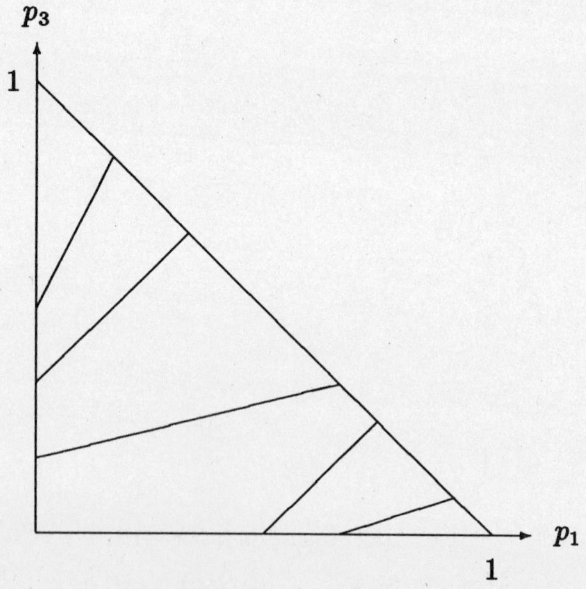

Straight indifference curves in L

Hence, dp_3/dp_1 is constant along the indifference curves. This implies that the numerator

$$\psi_2(x_2, 1-p_1) - \psi_2(x_1, 1-p_1)$$

of dp_3/dp_1 is constant. Now one can assume without loss of generality $x_1 = 0$ and that ψ is normalized such that $\psi(0,p) = 0$ for all $p \in [0,1]$ (see section 2.1). It follows that $\psi_2(x_2, 1-p_1)$ is a constant (depending only on x_2). Therefore ψ_2 is independent of the second argument. Thus, $\psi(x,p) = u(x)p + a$ for some $a \in \mathbf{R}$ and V is an expected utility functional.

Chapter 2

A Rank-Dependent Utility Model with Prize-Dependent Distortion of Probabilities

In this chapter a new model of choice under risk within the framework of RDU theory is offered. The suggested model contains the expected utility model as a special case. Compared to anticipated utility theory it is more general in one respect and more restrictive in another. It is more general since it allows the probability distortion to depend on the prizes available. But it restricts on the other hand these distortions to be homogeneous in the probabilities.

Section 2.1 reconsiders the formal structure of the general RDU model. It is shown that there corresponds to every RDU functional $V : D(X) \to \mathbf{R}$ a distinct function $v : X \times [0,1] \to \mathbf{R}$ unique up to a positive linear transformation such that V is determined by v and $v(x,p)$ can be interpreted as the *utility of winning x with probability p (and otherwise nothing).* Therefore, the function v is referred to as the *generalized utility function.* Furthermore, it is shown that the general RDU model can be substantially simplified in its technical aspects if the generalized utility function is assumed to be absolutely continuous. This assumption yields a very simple functional form of the extended representation on the set of all distribution functions on X. Absolute continuity of v corresponds to absolute continuity of the epigraph measure with respect to the Lebesgue measure.

In section 2.2 it is demonstrated how the assumption of homogeneity of v with respect to the second variable explains the empirical patterns exhibited by the Allais paradox and the common ratio effect. The results indicate that the homogeneous RDU model can cover these patterns in a very natural way.

Section 2.3 is devoted to the general issue of prize-dependent distortions of probabilities. The topic discussed there is closely related to the example in the introduction.

Section 2.4 characterizes the homogeneous RDU model using a numerical index – called the *relative utility index* – that relates the utility of winning x with some proportion q of the probability p to the utility of winning x with p.

The method developed in 2.4 is applied in section 2.5 to give new characterizations of the anticipated utility model, the dual theory and the expected utility model. It turns out that whereas the homogeneous RDU model corresponds to the case where relative utility is independent of p, the anticipated utility model requires the relative utility index to be independent of x. As another result it is shown that weighted linear utility theory together with the homogeneity condition implies expected utility maximizing behavior.

Finally, in section 2.6 a more general model within the RDU approach is presented containing both the homogeneous RDU model and the anticipated utility model as special cases. It is indicated that the generalized model could be advantageous in choice situations where the specific assumptions of the other approaches do not apply.

2.1 Rank-Dependent Utility Theory Reconsidered

2.1.1 The Generalized Utility Function

Let $\succeq$ be a binary relation on $D(X)$. Throughout this chapter it will be assumed that $\succeq$ is a continuous, (strictly) monotone weak order, i.e. $\succeq$ satisfies axioms 1,2 and 4. If $\succeq$ in addition satisfies ordinal independence (axiom 10) there exists by theorem 1.4.4 a function $\psi :$ $X \times [0,1] \to \mathbf{R}$ such that

$$F \mapsto \psi(x_1, 1) + \sum_{i=2}^{n} \left(\psi(x_i, \sum_{j=i}^{n} p_j) - \psi(x_{i-1}, \sum_{j=i}^{n} p_j) \right)$$

represents $\succeq$ on $D^0(X)$ where $F = (x_1; p_1, \ldots, x_n; p_n)$. Furthermore, ψ is continuous in each argument, $\psi(\cdot, 0) = 0$, and ψ satisfies condition (1.18).

It will now be shown that there exists a distinct such function ψ which allows for an intuitive interpretation. For this purpose define for a given ψ satisfying the condition above a function $v : X \times [0,1] \to \mathbf{R}$ by

$$v(x,p) = \psi(x,p) - \psi(0,p) \quad \text{for } (x,p) \in X \times [0,1].$$

Obviously, $v(\cdot, 0) = 0$, v is continuous in each argument and

$$v(y,q) - v(y,p) - v(x,q) + v(x,p) > 0 \quad \text{for } y > x, q > p.$$

It is also immediately verified that

$$V(F) = v(x_1, 1) + \sum_{i=2}^{n} \left(v(x_i, \sum_{j=i}^{n} p_j) - v(x_{i-1}, \sum_{j=i}^{n} p_j) \right) \tag{2.1}$$

is a representation of preferences with

$$V(\delta_0) = 0 \tag{2.2}$$

and

$$V((0;1-p,x;p)) = v(x,p) \quad \text{for all } (x,p) \in X \times [0,1]. \tag{2.3}$$

By the last equation, $v(x,p)$ can be interpreted as the *utility of winning x with probability p and otherwise nothing.* From now on a function v satisfying the conditions of the representation theorem 1.4.4 and in addition (2.2) and (2.3) will be referred to as a *generalized utility function.* Note that the generalized utility function completely determines the preference relation from which it is derived. Also observe that the corresponding representation is normalized by (2.2) such that the utility of winning zero with certainty is set to zero.

According to the considerations in section 1.4.5 there corresponds to every generalized utility function v a measure μ on $X \times [0,1]$ with

$$\mu([0,x] \times [1-p,1]) = v(x,p) \quad \text{for all } (x,p) \in X \times [0,1], \tag{2.4}$$

such that the area of the epigraph of a distribution function with respect to the measure μ represents the preferences from which v is derived. We emphasize again that a measure on $X \times [0,1]$, continuous in the sense of theorem 1.4.5, is determined by its values on the set of all closed rectangles in $X \times [0,1]$. By additivity the measure of an arbitrary closed rectangle is determined by the values of the measure on the set of all closed rectangles having their upper left corner at the point $(0,1)$. Thus, the generalized utility function uniquely determines the measure μ by equation (2.4). Note that, conversely, for every epigraph measure μ the function v defined by (2.4) is a generalized utility function.

The correspondence between generalized utility functions and epigraph measures is useful to prove the following lemma which asserts that the generalized utility function derived from an RDU functional $V : D(X) \to \mathbf{R}$ is unique up to a positive linear transformation.

Lemma 2.1.1 *Let $\succeq$ be a binary relation on $D(X)$ satisfying axioms 1,2,4 and 10. If v and v^* are generalized utility functions corresponding to $\succeq$ then there exists a $g \in \mathbf{R}^+$ such that $v^* = gv$.*

For the proof of lemma 2.1.1 we need the following result which will be useful also in section 2.4.

Lemma 2.1.2 *Suppose that $\tau : [0,m] \to \mathbf{R}$ is continuous and satisfies the functional equation*

$$\tau(w+z) = \tau(w) + \tau(z) \quad \textit{for all } w, z \in [0,m] \textit{ with } w+z \in [0,m].$$

Then there exists a $g \in \mathbf{R}$ such that $\tau(z) = gz$ for all $z \in [0,m]$.

Proof. Firstly, observe that τ can be extended to a function on $\mathbf{R}^+$ satisfying the functional equation. Then the lemma follows from [EICHHORN 1978, Corollary 1.3.7].

Proof of lemma 2.1.1. Let μ and μ^* be the epigraph measures corresponding to v and v^*, respectively. Since both measures represent $\succeq$ on $D(X)$ in the sense of (1.20) there exists a positive monotonic transformation $\tau : [0,m] \to \mathbf{R}$ such that

$$\mu^*(e_F) = \tau(\mu(e_F)) \quad \text{for all } F \in D(X),$$

where $m = \mu(X \times [0,1]) = v(M,1)$. Since the function $x \mapsto \mu^*([0,x] \times [0,1]) = v^*(x,1)$ is continuous, and the function $x \mapsto \mu([0,x] \times [0,1]) = v(x,1)$ takes by first-order stochastic dominance and (weak) continuity all values in $[0,m]$, the transformation τ must be continuous.

Since the measures μ and μ^* are both uniquely determined by their restriction to the set of all rectangles with upper left corner at $(0,1)$ one has $\mu^*(A) = \tau(\mu(A))$ for all subsets $A \subset X \times [0,1]$. For $w, z \in [0,m]$ with $w + z \in [0,m]$ choose disjoint subsets $A, B \subset X \times [0,1]$ such that $\mu(A) = w$ and $\mu(B) = z$. By additivity of μ and μ^*,

$$\tau(w+z) = \tau(\mu(A \cup B)) = \mu^*(A \cup B) =$$
$$\mu^*(A) + \mu^*(B) = \tau(\mu(A)) + \tau(\mu(B)) = \tau(w) + \tau(z),$$

hence $\tau(z) = gz$ for some $g > 0$ by lemma 2.1.2. Therefore $v^*(x,p) = gv(x,p)$ for all $(x,p) \in X \times [0,1]$.

2.1.2 Absolute Continuity

So far, nothing has been said about how the representation (2.1) can be extended from $D^0(X)$ to $D(X)$. It turns out that some additional assumptions are necessary to obtain such an extension in a satisfactory form.[1]

Here, it will be assumed that the epigraph measure corresponding to the preference relation is mutually *absolutely continuous* with respect to the Lebesgue measure.[2] Equivalently, one may assume that the corresponding generalized utility function v is absolutely continuous with respect to the first variable and that the derivative with respect to the first variable, denoted by v_1, in turn is absolutely continuous with respect to the second variable. This assumption implies that the extended representation takes the simple form

$$V(F) = \int_0^M v_1(x, 1 - F(x))dx \quad \text{for all } F \in D(X). \tag{2.5}$$

Moreover, the connection between the epigraph measure μ and the generalized utility function v is further specified by the equation

$$\mu(e_F) = \int_0^M \int_{F(x)}^1 v_{12}(x, 1 - \pi)d\pi dx, \tag{2.6}$$

where v_{12} denotes the derivative of v_1 with respect to the second variable. Thus, the function $(x,p) \mapsto v_{12}(x, 1-p)$ is the *Radon-Nikodym density* of the measure μ. Before we prove these results in detail an

[1]For an approach to this problem without further assumptions but with a considerable amount of technical details see the appendix of [Chew and Epstein 1989].

[2]The assumption of absolute continuity is much weaker than the condition of *differentiability on basic distributions* used in [Green and Jullien 1988].

example is given showing that the epigraph measure need not be absolutely continuous with respect to the Lebesgue measure.

Let $u : X \to \mathbf{R}$ with $u(0) = 0$ be continuous and strictly increasing but not absolutely continuous. For the existence of such a function see e.g. [NATANSON 1961, p.239] or [ROYDEN 1968, ch.5, problem 12]. Define μ to be the unique measure on $X \times [0,1]$ with $\mu([0,x] \times [1-p,1]) = u(x)p$ and a preference relation $\succeq$ by

$$F \succeq G \Leftrightarrow \mu(e_F) \geq \mu(e_G) \quad \text{for all } F, G \in D(X).$$

It is easy to verify that this binary relation satisfies axioms 1,2 and 4. Moreover, it satisfies the independence axiom and therefore clearly also the ordinal independence axiom. However, the epigraph measure μ is not absolutely continuous with respect to the Lebesgue measure. Since the epigraph measure is unique up to a positive linear transformation this is also true for any other epigraph measure representing the same preference relation.

Assume now that the epigraph measure μ corresponding to an RDU functional $V : D(X) \to \mathbf{R}$ is mutually absolutely continuous with respect to the Lebesgue measure, i.e. for every $A \subset X \times [0,1]$, $\mu(A) = 0$ if and only if A has Lebesgue measure zero. Then, by the Radon-Nikodym theorem (see e.g. [ROYDEN 1968, ch.11]) there exists an integrable function $\rho : X \times [0,1] \to \mathbf{R}$ such that for every measurable set $A \subset X \times [0,1]$,

$$\mu(A) = \int_A \rho(z,\pi) d\pi dz.$$

In particular, for $A = [0,x] \times [1-p,1]$ one obtains

$$\begin{aligned} v(x,p) &= \mu([0,x] \times [1-p,1]) \\ &= \int_0^x \int_{1-p}^1 \rho(z,\pi) d\pi dz \\ &= \int_0^x \left(\int_0^p \rho(z, 1-\pi) d\pi \right) dz. \end{aligned}$$

Since $v(\cdot, p)$ is an indefinite integral it is absolutely continuous and its derivative $v_1(\cdot, p)$ equals $\int_0^p \rho(\cdot, 1-\pi)d\pi$ almost everywhere [ROYDEN 1968, theorem 4.13]. But the derivative is again an indefinite integral, thus v_1 may be chosen in such a way that $v_1(x, \cdot)$ is absolutely continuous with derivative $v_{12}(x, \cdot) = \rho(x, 1 - \cdot)$ almost everywhere.

Since the Lebesgue measure is assumed to be absolutely continuous with respect to μ the Radon-Nikodym density may be chosen positive in the interior of $X \times [0,1]$. Thus, $v_{12} > 0$ in the interior of $X \times [0,1]$ and consequently $v_1(x, \cdot)$ is strictly increasing for every $x \in X \setminus \{0\}$.

Summarizing, for every binary relation $\succeq$ satisfying axioms 1,2,4 and 10 such that the corresponding epigraph measure is mutually absolutely continuous with respect to the Lebesgue measure there exists a generalized utility function v with the following property.

Property 1 *The function* $v : X \times [0,1] \to \mathbf{R}$ *satisfies*

(i) $v = 0$ *on the set* $\mathcal{B} := (X \times \{0\}) \cup (\{0\} \times [0,1])$ *and*

(ii) v *is absolutely continuous with respect to the first variable. The derivative* v_1 *(in the sense that* $v_1 = \partial v / \partial x$ *almost everywhere) can be chosen in such a way that* v_1 *is absolutely continuous with respect to the second variable and* $v_1(x, \cdot)$ *is strictly increasing for every* $x \in X \setminus \{0\}$.

Furthermore, $\succeq$ is represented by (2.5) on $D(X)$ which reduces to (2.1) if $F \in D^0(X)$.

The following theorem shows that property 1 is not only a necessary but also a sufficient condition for a function v to be the generalized utility function of an RDU functional provided that the corresponding epigraph measure is mutually absolutely continuous with respect to the Lebesgue measure. (A version of this theorem was firstly proved in [PUPPE 1990a]).

Theorem 2.1.3 *Let* $\succeq$ *be a binary relation on* $D(X)$. *Then* $\succeq$ *satisfies axioms 1,2,4 and 10 with the corresponding epigraph measure being* *mutually absolutely continuous with respect to the Lebesgue measure if and only if there exists a function v with property 1 such that*

$$V(F) = \int_0^M v_1(x, 1 - F(x))dx$$

is a representation of $\succeq$ *on* $D(X)$.

Proof. The "only if" part has been proved above. Note that the representation given in the theorem is the continuous extension of (2.1) to $D(X)$.

Conversely, let v be a function with property 1 representing $\succeq$ as in the theorem. Obviously, $\succeq$ is a weak order. It is also immediately verified that $\succeq$ satisfies ordinal independence as a consequence of the existence of an integral representation. To prove the continuity of $\succeq$, let F_n be a sequence in $D(X)$ converging weakly to $F \in D(X)$, i.e. $F_n(x) \to F(x)$ at every continuity point x of F. The set of discontinuity points of F has Lebesgue measure zero. Therefore, since $v_1(x, \cdot)$ is continuous, the sequence $v_1(x, 1 - F_n(x))$ converges almost everywhere to $v_1(x, 1 - F(x))$. By the dominated convergence theorem $V(F_n) \to V(F)$, hence V is continuous and so is $\succeq$.

To prove monotonicity of $\succeq$, let F dominate G by first-order stochastic dominance, i.e. $F(x) \leq G(x)$ on X with strict inequality for at least one $x_0 \in X$. By right-hand continuity of F and G there exists an $\epsilon > 0$ such that $F < G$ on $[x_0, x_0 + \epsilon)$ and without loss of generality we may assume $x_0 \neq 0$. Then $V(F) > V(G)$ follows immediately from the fact that in the representation v_1 is strictly increasing in the second variable.

Finally, we note that the epigraph measure μ corresponding to $\succeq$ is given by equation (2.6). Thus, since μ has a density it must be absolutely continuous with respect to the Lebesgue measure. On the other hand, by property 1(ii) the density function may be chosen positive on $(X \times [0,1]) \setminus \mathcal{B}$ and therefore the Lebesgue measure is also absolutely continuous with respect to μ.

2.1.3 The Set of Elementary Lotteries

Theorem 2.1.3 may be interpreted as a *completeness property* of the general RDU model with respect to behavior on the set of lotteries of the form $(0; 1-p, x; p)$. To explain this idea let $D^{el}(X)$ denote the set consisting of all lotteries with two outcomes one of which is always zero. Thus,

$$D^{el}(X) = \{(0; 1-p, x; p) : (x, p) \in X \times [0, 1]\}.$$

This set will be referred to as the set of *elementary lotteries*. Note that for an elementary lottery $F = (0; 1-p, x, p)$ the epigraph e_F is the set $[0, x] \times [1-p, 1]$.

The RDU model may be described as a model where the preference between arbitrary distributions is determined by a *cardinal utility* on the set $D^{el}(X)$. This cardinal utility is what we have called the generalized utility function. One may ask then which functions v are admissible as generalized utility functions. Obviously, since for $(x, p) \in \mathcal{B} = (X \times \{0\}) \cup (\{0\} \times [0, 1])$ the lotteries $(0; 1-p, x; p)$ represent the same distribution giving zero with certainty, v should be constant on $\mathcal{B}$ and by normalization equal to zero there. The monotonicity of preferences restricted to $D^{el}(X)$ implies that v should be a strictly increasing function of x for every fixed $p \neq 0$ and of p for every fixed $x \neq 0$. Note that the monotonicity of v in each variable follows from property 1. Thus, by theorem 2.1.3 there is (besides the regularity conditions) only one additional property needed to ensure that the preference relation satisfies the principle of first-order stochastic dominance on $D(X)$. The property is that v_1 should be a strictly increasing function of the second variable. This property is the only condition which cannot be interpreted from the viewpoint of v as a cardinal utility on $D^{el}(X)$.

These considerations allow to study a variety of different forms of the generalized utility function within the framework of RDU theory not necessarily implying multiplicative separability as in the anticipated utility model. One such form leading to plausible explanations of observed phenomena is examined in the remaining sections of this chapter.

2.2 Homogeneity on Elementary Lotteries

In this section a special functional form of the generalized utility function is suggested. It will be assumed in the sequel that v is *homogeneous in the probability.* Unlike in expected utility theory where the degree of homogeneity is equal to 1, or in anticipated utility where the degree of homogeneity may differ from 1 but must be constant, no further restrictions are imposed here. Thus, the generalized utility function takes the form

$$v(x,p) = \begin{cases} u(x)p^{g(x)} & \text{if } p \neq 0 \\ 0 & \text{if } p = 0. \end{cases} \tag{2.7}$$

To avoid technical difficulties not essential to the approach taken here it will be assumed in the sequel that the functions $u : X \to \mathbf{R}$ and $g : X \to \mathbf{R}$ are continuously differentiable on X. The conditions guaranteeing the function v in (2.7) to be a generalized utility function are as follows. Firstly, by property 1(i) v must vanish on the set $\mathcal{B}$, hence $u(0) = 0$. By first-order stochastic dominance u is strictly increasing and $g > 0$. By property 1(ii) the derivative v_1 must be strictly increasing in the propbability p. The derivative v_1 is given by

$$v_1(x,p) = \begin{cases} (u'(x) + u(x)g'(x)\ln p)p^{g(x)} & \text{if } p \neq 0 \\ 0 & \text{if } p = 0. \end{cases}$$

Differentiation[3] with respect to the second variable yields

$$v_{12}(x,p) = ((ug)'(x) + u(x)g(x)g'(x)\ln p)p^{g(x)-1}.$$

The function v_{12} is positive in the interior of $X \times [0,1]$ (except possibly at isolated points) if g is non-increasing and the product ug is strictly increasing. Summarizing, the following assumption will be made.

Assumption 2 *The functions $u : X \to \mathbf{R}$ and $g : X \to \mathbf{R}$ satisfy the conditions $u(0) = 0$, $g > 0$, u is strictly increasing, g is non-increasing and the product $ug : X \to \mathbf{R}$ is strictly increasing.*

The interpretation of (2.7) as a generalized utility function is as follows. For fixed $x \in X$ there may be a subjective underestimation or a subjective overestimation of the probability with which x is received, depending on the sign of $g(x) - 1$. But by virtue of g being non-increasing there is a tendency to weaken the underestimation or strengthen the overestimation, respectively, if x increases. Hence, the functional form of (2.7) captures in some way an *optimistic* attitude towards risk: No matter how an individual initially estimates the probability p of winning the prize x, raising the prize leads in any case to a higher estimation of the corresponding probability. It is clear that this effect may cause a substantial distortion especially of low probabilities if high prizes are at stake. Thus, the functional form (2.7) of the generalized utility function explains the widely observed inclination to participate in gambles offering high prizes with a very low probability not by the high utility of large gains but by an optimistic attitude towards gambling if the possible outcomes are large. It is worth noting that this kind of optimism does not rule out risk aversion at the same time. Therefore, the optimistic attitude exhibited by (2.7) should not

[3]Note that $v_1(x,\cdot)$ is continuous for every $x \in X$ since $(\ln p)p^{g(x)} \to 0$ for $p \to 0$, and $v_1(x,\cdot)$ is differentiable for $p \in (0,1]$.

be taken for *risk loving* behavior. This point will be further discussed in chapter 3.

It will now be shown that the optimism towards gambling exhibited by the generalized utility function (2.7) can serve as an explanation of the common ratio effect and the Allais paradox.

2.2.1 The Common Ratio Effect

Consider again the lotteries c_i for $i = 1, ..., 4$ of section 1.3. Recall that c_1 and c_2 are the elementary lotteries offering the chance of winning x with probability p and y with probability q, respectively, where $0 < x < y$ and $0 < q < p$. The lotteries c_3 and c_4 are derived from c_1 and c_2 by multiplying the corresponding probabilities by the common factor $r \in (0, 1)$.

The explanation for the choice of c_1 in the first pair and of c_4 in the second pair suggested here – in accordance with the functional form (2.7) of the generalized utility function – is that the relatively small probability rq in c_4 is subject to a relatively strong overestimation resulting from the higher prize y. The same effect may occur of course also in c_2 but will be weaker since the corresponding probability is greater. Formally, the following theorem applies (see also [PUPPE 1990a]).

Theorem 2.2.1 *For any given set $\{x, y, p, q, r\}$ of parameters with $0 < x < y \leq M$, $0 < q < p \leq 1$ and $r \in (0, 1)$ and for any strictly increasing utility function $u : X \to \mathbf{R}$ with $u(0) = 0$ there exists a function $g : X \to \mathbf{R}$ such that assumption 2 is fulfilled and such that for an RDU functional V with generalized utility function $v(x, p) = u(x)p^{g(x)}$ one has*

$$V(c_1) > V(c_2) \quad \text{and} \quad V(c_3) < V(c_4).$$

Proof. Two positive numbers g_x and g_y with constant difference $k_1 :=$

$g_x - g_y > 0$ will be determined as follows. For

$$\gamma := \frac{u(x)p^{g_x}}{u(y)q^{g_y}}$$

it follows that

$$\ln \gamma = \ln \frac{u(x)}{u(y)} + (\ln p)(g_x - g_y) + g_y(\ln p - \ln q).$$

For suitable positive constants k_2, k_3 one has therefore $\ln \gamma = -k_2 + g_y k_3$. By this last expression $\ln \gamma$ depends continuously on g_y, takes negative values for small positive g_y and positive values for large g_y. Now choose g_y such that $\ln \gamma > 0$, and

$$r < e^{-\frac{\ln \gamma}{k_1}}.$$

Choose then a positive decreasing function $g : X \to \mathbf{R}$ with $g(x) = g_x$ and $g(y) = g_y$. Since k_1 may be arbitrarily small g can be chosen such that ug is strictly increasing, so that assumption 2 is satisfied. The proof is complete by noting that the construction of g implies $V(c_1) > V(c_2)$ and $V(c_3) < V(c_4)$.

The theorem shows that under the hypothesis of homogeneity in the probability the choices observed in connection with the common ratio effect are consistent with *any* strictly increasing utility function. We turn now to the Allais paradox.

2.2.2 The Allais Paradox

The explanation for the behavior exhibited by the Allais paradox is of course similar to our account of the common ratio effect. Consider the lotteries $a_1, ..., a_4$ of section 1.3. Here, it is the probability 0.1 corresponding to the prize \$5,000,000 in a_4 which is disproportionately overweighted to yield the choice of a_4 in the second pair although a_1 is preferred in the first pair. In contrast to the common ratio effect, however, not only the distortion function g must be suitably specified to yield consistency with the Allais paradox but also the utility function.

The consistency of the functional form (2.7) with Allais type behavior will be proved for a slightly more general pattern as the original Allais paradox. For this purpose the following two pairs of lotteries are considered, where it is assumed that $y > x$.

$$\tilde{a}_1 : \{1.00 \text{ chance of DM } x \quad \text{versus} \quad \tilde{a}_2 : \begin{cases} 0.10 \text{ chance of DM } y \\ 0.89 \text{ chance of DM } x \\ 0.01 \text{ chance of DM } 0 \end{cases}$$

and

$$\tilde{a}_3 : \begin{cases} 0.11 \text{ chance of DM } x \\ 0.89 \text{ chance of DM } 0 \end{cases} \quad \text{versus} \quad \tilde{a}_4 : \begin{cases} 0.10 \text{ chance of DM } y \\ 0.90 \text{ chance of DM } 0 \end{cases}$$

Theorem 2.2.2 *For any given x, y with $M \geq y > x > 0$ there exist functions u, g satisfying assumption 2 such that $V(\tilde{a}_1) > V(\tilde{a}_2)$ and $V(\tilde{a}_3) < V(\tilde{a}_4)$ for the RDU functional V corresponding to the generalized utility function $v(x,p) = u(x)p^{g(x)}$.*

Proof. (See also [PUPPE 1990a].) Set $u_y = 2u_x$ and $g_x = g_y + u_x$; if u_x and g_y become sufficiently large it follows that

$$u_y(0.1)^{g_y} > u_x(0.11)^{g_x}$$

and

$$u_x > u_x(0.99)^{g_x} + u_y(0.1)^{g_y} - u_x(0.1)^{g_x}.$$

Choose u, g according to assumption 2 with $u(x) = u_x$, $u(y) = u_y$, $g(x) = g_x$ and $g(y) = g_y$. The proof is complete by noting that the constuction implies a preference for $\tilde{a}_1$ over $\tilde{a}_2$ and for $\tilde{a}_4$ over $\tilde{a}_3$.

2.3 Further Evidence for Prize-Dependent Distortions of Probabilities

Since the behavior exhibited by the Allais paradox and the common ratio effect is consistent not only with the hypothesis of homogeneity in the probability of the generalized utility function but also with anticipated utility theory the results of the previous section can not serve as an ultimate justification of considering prize-dependent distortions of probabilities rather than *uniform*, i.e. prize-independent, distortions.

In this section we try to explore the intuition that the prizes at stake may influence the perception of the relevant probabilities, thus implying prize-dependent distortions of probabilities. Recall the hungry individual described in the introduction by the preferences

$$(\$5; 1) \succ (\$0; 0.99, \$500; 0.01) \tag{2.8}$$

and

$$(\$500; 1) \prec (\$0; 0.99, \$50,000; 0.01). \tag{2.9}$$

The explanation of these preferences given in the introduction was that the individual perceived the probability 0.01 in the second pair in a different way than in the first pair because of the higher prize $50,000. The conclusion that the individual exhibits prize-dependent distortions of probabilities follows of course only under additional assumptions about the utility function $u : X \to \mathbf{R}$. If, for instance, u is linear, i.e. $u(x) = x$ for all $x \in X$, then (2.8) and (2.9) imply the non-existence of a uniform distortion function $f : [0,1] \to [0,1]$ such that preferences among elementary lotteries are represented by $xf(p)$.

Alternatively, one may model the choices (2.8) and (2.9) by a specific (non-linear) shape of the utility function while maintaining a representation with uniform distortions of probabilities.

The issue raised by the example is not that the choices (2.8),(2.9) *imply* prize-dependent distortions of probabilities but rather that this hypothesis makes (2.8) and (2.9) consistent with *any* strictly increasing utility function $u : X \to \mathbf{R}$. The same is obviously not true of the anticipated utility model which, given (2.8) and (2.9), rules out not only a linear utility function but e.g. any utility function of the form $u(x) = x^t$ for $t > 0$.

The same idea is expressed in the following lemma in a slightly different way.

Lemma 2.3.1 *Suppose an individual has a strictly increasing utility function* $u : X \to \mathbf{R}$ *with* $u(0) = 0$. *Let* $y \in X \setminus \{0\}$ *and* $p \in (0,1)$ *be such that*

$$(0; 1-p, M; p) \succ (y; 1).$$

Then there always exists a $x \in (0, y)$ *(depending on* u*) such that*

$$(0; 1-p, y; p) \prec (x; 1)$$

implies prize-dependent distortions of probabilities.

Proof. Suppose that the individual performs a uniform distortion of the probabilities, i.e anticipated utility theory applies. Without loss of generality we may assume $u(M) = 1$. Then the first preference comparison implies $f(p) > u(y)$. Define $x \in (0, y)$ by $x = u^{-1}(u(y)^2)$. It follows that $f(p)u(y) > u(y)^2 = u(x)$ and thus $(0; 1-p, y; p) \succ (x; 1)$. Thus, for the chosen x the choices presumed in the lemma rule out the possibility of a uniform distortion of probabilities.

2.4 A Characterization Theorem

In this section a characterization theorem for the homogeneous RDU model is proved. The characterization is not obtained by an additional axiom imposed directly on the preference relation but in terms of a specific property of the generalized utility function (2.7).

Let $V : D(X) \to \mathbf{R}$ be an RDU functional with corresponding generalized utility function $v : X \times [0,1] \to \mathbf{R}$. For $(x,p) \notin \mathcal{B}$ and every $r \in [0,1]$ define a function $\varrho_r : (X \times [0,1]) \setminus \mathcal{B} \to \mathbf{R}$ by

$$\varrho_r(x,p) = \frac{v(x,rp)}{v(x,p)}. \tag{2.10}$$

This function reflects the utility of winning x with some proportion r of the probability p relative to the utility of winning x with p. Therefore, ϱ_r is referred to as the *relative utility index corresponding to the proportion* r. Note that by the uniqueness property of the generalized utility function this index does not depend on the choice of the function v.

The following theorem shows that a generalized utility function is homogeneous in the probability if and only if the corresponding relative utility indices are independent of the probability p (see also [PUPPE 1990b]).

Theorem 2.4.1 *Let $\succeq$ be a preference relation on $D(X)$ satisfying axioms 1,2,4 and 10. Then the corresponding generalized utility function v is homogeneous in p, i.e. $v(x,p) = u(x)p^{g(x)}$ for suitable functions u and g satisfying assumption 2, if and only if for every $r \in [0,1]$ the relative utility index ϱ_r is independent of p.*

Proof. Obviously, if the generalized utility function is homogeneous the relative utility indices are independent of p.

Let now conversely ϱ_r be independent of p for all r; then

$$\frac{v(x,rp)}{v(x,p)} = \frac{v(x,r)}{v(x,1)}$$

for all $p \in (0,1]$. If $v(x,1)$ is denoted by $u(x)$ it follows that $u(0) = 0$, u is strictly increasing and

$$\ln u(x) + \ln v(x,rp) = \ln v(x,r) + \ln v(x,p).$$

The substitution $p = e^{-z}$ and $r = e^{-w}$ for $z, w \in [0, \infty)$ implies

$$\ln u(x) + \ln v(x, e^{-w-z}) = \ln v(x, e^{-w}) + \ln v(x, e^{-z}).$$

Now apply lemma 2.1.2 to the function $\tau_x(z) := \ln v(x, e^{-z}) - \ln u(x)$ to obtain $\tau_x(z) = -g(x)z$ for some $g(x) > 0$. Hence,

$$\ln v(x, e^{-z}) = -g(x)z + \ln u(x),$$

and therefore

$$\ln v(x, p) = g(x) \ln p + \ln u(x) = \ln(u(x)p^{g(x)}),$$

so finally $v(x, p) = u(x)p^{g(x)}$ is obtained.

2.5 Rank-Dependent Utility Theory and Relative Utility

In this section the various specializations of the RDU approach (see the figure at the end of this chapter) other than the homogeneous case are characterized by means of the relative utility index (2.10). The dual theory may be characterized using a "dual" relative utility index which relates the utility of winning a certain proportion r of the amount x with probability p to the utility of winning x with p.

It turns out that anticipated utility theory is in some sense "dual" to the homogeneous case. It is characterized by the fact that the relative utility index is independent of the prize x or, equivalently, that the dual index is independent of the probability p.

Finally, it is shown that weighted linear utility theory together with the condition that the relative utility index is independent of p implies expected utility maximization. Thus, in contrast to the ordinal independence axiom the weak substitution axiom forces any homogeneity on elementary lotteries to be of degree 1.

It will be convenient to assume $X = [0,1]$ for the rest of this chapter. This is no restriction since one can think of a prize $x \in [0,1]$ as a proportion of the fixed amount M. Let $V : D(X) \to \mathbf{R}$ be an RDU functional with corresponding generalized utility function v. For $(x,p) \in (X \times [0,1]) \setminus \mathcal{B}$ and $r \in [0,1]$ define the *dual relative utility index* by

$$\tilde{\varrho}_r(x,p) = \frac{v(rx,p)}{v(x,p)}. \tag{2.11}$$

As the index (2.10) this index does not depend on the choice of the function v. The following theorem gives necessary and sufficient conditions for a preference relation on $D(X)$ to be representable by an anticipated utility functional.

Theorem 2.5.1 *Let $\succeq$ be a binary relation on $D(X)$. The following conditions are equivalent.*

(i) *There exist continuous and strictly increasing functions $u : X \to \mathbf{R}$, unique up to a positive linear transformation, and $f : [0,1] \to [0,1]$, unique, with $u(0) = 0$, f surjective such that*

$$F \mapsto -\int_X u(x)df(1-F(x)) \quad \textit{for all } F \in D(X)$$

represents $\succeq$.

(ii) *The relation $\succeq$ satisfies axioms 1,2,4 and 10, and for any $r \in [0,1]$ the corresponding relative utility index (2.10) is independent of x.*

(iii) *The relation $\succeq$ satisfies axioms 1,2,4 and 10, and for any $r \in [0,1]$ the corresponding dual index (2.11) is independent of p.*

Proof. It is easy to verify "(i) $\Rightarrow$ (ii),(iii)". Now suppose (ii) holds. Let ϱ be the relative utility index corresponding to $\succeq$. Since ϱ_r is independent of x one has

$$\frac{v(x,rp)}{v(x,p)} = l(r,p)$$

for a suitable function $l : X \times (0,1] \to \mathbf{R}$. In particular, for $p = 1$

$$\frac{v(x,r)}{v(x,1)} = l(r,1).$$

With the notation $u(x) := v(x,1)$ and $f(r) := l(r,1)$ one obtains $v(x,p) = u(x)f(p)$. Obviously, $u(0) = 0$, $f(0) = 0$, $f(1) = 1$ and u, f are continuous and strictly increasing. The anticipated utility representation follows immediately from the representation (2.1) or from (2.5) when integrating by parts. Thus, (i) holds.

Assume now (iii) and let $\tilde{\varrho}$ be the dual relative utility index corresponding to $\succeq$. Since $\tilde{\varrho}_r$ is independent of p one has

$$\frac{v(rx,p)}{v(x,p)} = \tilde{l}(r,x).$$

Using the notation $f(p) := v(1,p)/v(1,1)$ and $u(x) := v(1,1)\tilde{l}(x,1)$ it is immediately verified that $v(x,p) = u(x)f(p)$ with continuous, strictly increasing functions u, f, and thus (i) follows as before.

The theorem above shows that the anticipated utility model is in some sense "dual" to the homogeneous model within the framework of RDU theory. Whereas in the homogeneous RDU model the index ϱ may vary with x in anticipated utility theory it varies only with p or, equivalently, the dual index $\tilde{\varrho}$ varies with x. It is interesting to remark that at least one of this conditions must hold in an RDU model which is consistent with the common ratio effect. Indeed, suppose that ϱ_r is for all r independent of both x and p. The resulting RDU model has a generalized utility function $v(x,p) = u(x)p^t$ for some constant $t > 0$. Obviously, in that case the choice of c_1 in the first pair of lotteries in the common ratio effect (see section 1.3) implies the choice of c_3 in the second pair, thus contradicting the observed behavior. Consequently, the common ratio effect rules out not merely expected utility maximizing behavior – which corresponds to $v(x,p) = u(x)p$ –

but any RDU model for which the corresponding relative utility index is independent of both x and p.[4]

It is worth emphasizing that the condition of ϱ being independent of x and p is – although necessary – not sufficient for expected utility maximizing behavior. Expected utility theory implies for all r the relative utility index to be exactly equal to r. Thus, expected utility maximizing behavior is within RDU theory characterized by the requirement that the "proportion of utility" yielded by some proportion r of the probability is exactly equal to r.

A "dual" result holds for the dual theory of choice.

Theorem 2.5.2 *Let $\succeq$ be a binary relation on $D(X)$. Then $\succeq$ admits a dual representation (1.17) if and only if $\succeq$ satisfies axioms 1,2,4 and 10 and for any $r \in [0,1]$ the dual relative utility index (2.11) satisfies*

$$\tilde{\varrho}_r(x,p) = r \quad \textit{for all } (x,p) \in (X \times [0,1]) \setminus \mathcal{B}.$$

Proof. Obviously, the existence of a dual representation implies the stated properties. Let conversely $V : D(X) \to \mathbf{R}$ be an RDU representation of $\succeq$ with corresponding generalized utility function v normalized such that $v(1,1) = 1$. Then the condition on the dual relative utility index implies $v(rx,p) = rv(x,p)$ and in particular $v(r,p) = rv(1,p)$. Define $f(p) := v(1,p)$ to conclude that $v(x,p) = xf(p)$ with a continuous, strictly increasing and surjective function $f : [0,1] \to [0,1]$.

The section is concluded with a comparison of the homogeneous RDU model and weighted linear utility theory. It turns out that adding the homogeneity condition reduces the weighted linear utility model to expected utility theory.

[4]The class of RDU functionals which are both, multiplicatively separable and homogeneous, has been studied in [Segal 1987b] in context with the *Ellsberg paradox*.

Theorem 2.5.3 *Let $\succeq$ be a binary relation on $D(X)$ which satisfies axioms 1,2 and 4. The following conditions are equivalent.*

(i) *$\succeq$ satisfies independence (axiom 3).*

(ii) *$\succeq$ satisfies weak substitution (axiom 5) and for all $r \in [0,1]$ the relative utility index ϱ_r does not depend on p.*

Proof. It is clear that "(i) $\Rightarrow$ (ii)". Let conversely $w : X \to \mathbf{R}$ be a positive weight function such that the representation

$$F \mapsto \frac{\sum_{i=1}^{n} u(x_i)w(x_i)p_i}{\sum_{i=1}^{n} w(x_i)p_i}$$

applies for some strictly increasing utility function $u : X \to \mathbf{R}$ with $u(0) = 0$ and every $F = (x_1; p_1, ..., x_n; p_n)$. It follows that

$$\varrho_r(x,p) = \frac{r(w(0)(1-p) + w(x)p)}{w(0)(1-rp) + w(x)rp}.$$

Thus $\partial\varrho_r/\partial p = 0$ if and only if $(w(x) - w(0))(1-r)r = 0$ which is possible for all $r \in [0,1]$ if and only if w is constant. But in that case weighted linear utility theory reduces to expected utility theory. Hence, $\succeq$ satisfies the independence axiom.

2.6 A Generalized Model

In the previous section it was shown that the various specializations of the general RDU approach can be distinguished by the specific shapes of the corresponding relative utility indices. It turned out that all theories so far presented involve rather restrictive conditions concerning this shape. In this section these results will be further discussed. It will be argued in the sequel that there may be circumstances in which none of these conditions apply. Therefore, a more general model within the framework of RDU theory is considered to cover also these circumstances.

Consider firstly the condition (iii) of theorem 2.5.1 which characterizes anticipated utility theory. If it is true that small probabilities are disproportionately overweighted,[5] especially when large outcomes are at stake, then the (relative) overestimation of the probability p in the denominator of $\tilde{\varrho}_r(x,p) = v(rx,p)/v(x,p)$ will be stronger than the (relative) overestimation of the same probability in the numerator. But as p increases this effect will become weaker and weaker. Thus, it turns out that $\tilde{\varrho}_r$ should be an increasing function of p for all $r \in (0,1)$.[6] In the sequel we will examine the following hypothesis.

Hypothesis 3 *For every $r \in (0,1)$ and every $x \in (0,1]$ the dual relative utility index $\tilde{\varrho}_r$ is a strictly increasing function of p.*

Consider now the condition on the relative utility index (2.10) characterizing the homogeneous RDU model, namely that ϱ_r is independent of p for all r. Suppose that for a fixed r the probability p of winning x becomes very small. Then the index ϱ_r involves the comparison of two lotteries with very small probabilities. It could be argued that in the extreme case the utility of the lottery $(0;1-p,x;p)$ becomes indistinguishable from the utility of the lottery $(0;1-rp,x;rp)$. Consequently, the relative utility index should be close to 1. But as p increases the role of r becomes, at least psychological, more and more important. Hence, the ratio $v(x,rp)/v(x,p)$ becomes smaller as p increases. Thus the relative utility index should be a decreasing function of p.

Hypothesis 4 *For every $r \in (0,1)$ and every $x \in (0,1]$ the relative utility index ϱ_r is a strictly decreasing function of p.*

[5] This was found by many researchers (see e.g. [Preston and Baratta 1948] and the literature cited in chapter 1).

[6] In fact, for some classes of generalized utility functions the assumption of $\tilde{\varrho}_r$ being strictly *decreasing* with p would imply violations of first-order stochastic dominance. An example of such a generalized utility function is the homogeneous function (2.7).

By theorem 2.5.1 it follows that hypothesis 3 is incompatible with anticipated utility theory, and by theorem 2.4.1 hypothesis 4 rules out the possibility of a homogeneous representation. This observation suggests to consider a more general form of the generalized utility function which is compatible with both hypotheses at the same time.

Consider therefore a generalized utility function $v : X \times [0,1] \rightarrow \mathbf{R}$ of the following form (see also [PUPPE 1990c]).

$$v(x,p) = u(x)[f(p)]^{g(x)} \quad \text{for } (x,p) \in X \times [0,1], \tag{2.12}$$

where the functions $u, g : X \rightarrow \mathbf{R}$ and $f : [0,1] \rightarrow [0,1]$ satisfy the following set of conditions.

Assumption 5 *The functions u, f are continuous and strictly increasing with $u(0) = f(0) = 0$ and $f(1) = 1$, the function g is strictly positive and non-increasing, and the product $ug : X \rightarrow \mathbf{R}$ is strictly increasing.*

The following theorem gives necessary and sufficient conditions under which an RDU functional with generalized utility function of the form (2.12) satisfies the hypotheses 3 and 4.

Theorem 2.6.1 *Let $\succeq$ be a binary relation on $D(X)$ which satisfies axioms 1,2,4 and 10. Suppose that the corresponding generalized utility function is of the form (2.12) with $f : [0,1] \rightarrow [0,1]$ differentiable. Then*

(i) *Hypothesis 3 holds if and only if g is strictly decreasing.*

(ii) *Hypothesis 4 holds if and only if f displays strictly increasing elasticity.*

Before the proof is given it is interesting to note that the condition of strictly increasing elasticity of f is exactly the condition used in

[SEGAL 1987a] to show that anticipated utility theory is consistent with the behavior exhibited by the common ratio effect (see section 1.4). The condition in part (i) of theorem 2.6.1 ensures on the other hand that the corresponding RDU functional can not be reduced to an anticipated utility functional.

Proof of theorem 2.6.1. **(i)** Hypothesis 3 is equivalent to the function $f(p)^{g(rx)-g(x)}$ being strictly increasing in p for every $r \in (0,1)$ and $x \in (0,1]$. It is then straightforward to show that this condition is equivalent to $g(rx) > g(x)$ for every $r \in (0,1)$ and $x \in (0,1]$. Thus, it is equivalent to g being strictly decreasing.
(ii) Hypothesis 4 is equivalent to

$$\frac{d}{dp}\left(\frac{f(rp)}{f(p)}\right) < 0$$

for every $r \in (0,1)$ which is in turn equivalent to

$$\frac{rpf'(rp)}{f(rp)} < \frac{pf'(p)}{f(p)}.$$

The latter condition just asserts that the elasticity of f is strictly increasing.

The section is concluded with the following diagramm showing the interdependence of the various special cases of the RDU approach which have been considered here.

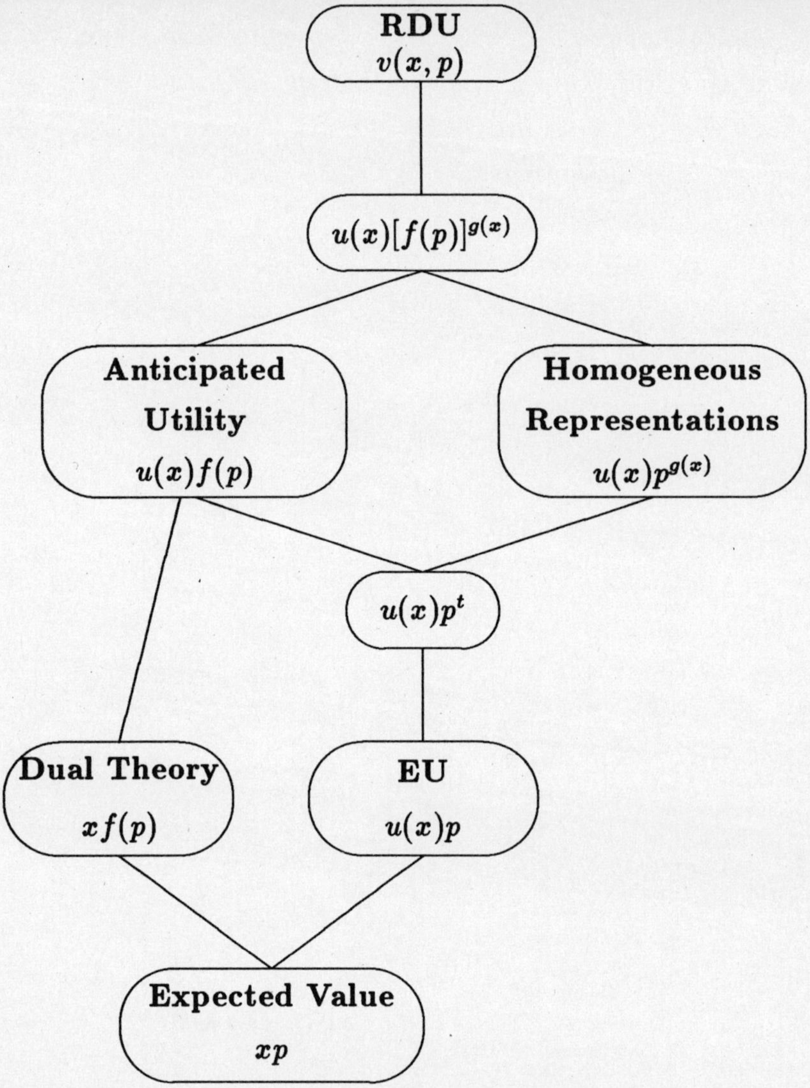

Rank-dependent specializations

Chapter 3

Risk Aversion

This chapter addresses the question under which conditions an RDU maximizer can be said to display *risk aversion.* Two concepts of risk aversion will be considered here. The first concept defines an individual to be risk averse if the sure gain $E(F)$ of the expectation of a distribution F is always preferred to the distribution itself. An alternative definition of risk aversion, suggested by ROTHSCHILD and STIGLITZ [1970], requires a risk averse individual to prefer a distribution F to any mean preserving spread of F. Obviously, a risk averter in the second sense is also risk averse in the sense of the first definition. It is well-known that in expected utility theory both concepts of risk aversion are equivalent to the concavity of the v.Neumann-Morgenstern utility function. However, the equivalence of the two notions of risk aversion does not carry over to general non-expected utility theories.

Section 3.1 gives a characterization of aversion to any mean preserving spread for the general RDU model. The analysis rests on the assumption that the preferences are representable by an RDU functional which is Gâteaux differentiable. Under this assumption the results of MACHINA [1982] and their extension by CHEW, KARNI and SAFRA [1987] can be used to obtain a simple characterization of risk aversion and comparative risk aversion in terms of the partial derivatives of the generalized utility function.

The fact that the two definitions of risk aversion do not coincide in RDU theory is illustrated in section 3.2. It is shown that an individual with a homogeneous generalized utility function will never be averse to *every* mean preserving spread unless the degree of homogeneity is constant. But in that case the assumption of homogeneity just yields a special case of anticipated utility theory. On the other hand, it is proved that an individual with a generalized utility function displaying prize-dependent distortion of probabilities can be strictly risk averse in the sense of the first definition even if the utility function is not strictly concave. Thus, as the dual theory the hypothesis of homogeneity in the probabilities allows to separate to some extent the notions of risk aversion and diminishing marginal utility of wealth.

In section 3.3 the notion of *decreasing* risk aversion is discussed. There, an important conceptual difference between the general RDU approach and the special cases of anticipated utility theory and the dual theory is explored. It turns out that whereas in anticipated utility theory the notion of decreasing absolute risk aversion in the sense of Arrow and Pratt depends only on properties of the corresponding utility function $u : X \rightarrow \mathbf{R}$, this is no longer true for the general RDU model. Thus, only the general RDU model allows to separate the notion of decreasing absolute risk aversion from attitudes towards wealth. Note that the dual theory assumes constant absolute risk aversion.

Finally, in section 3.4 the consequences of the preceding analysis on the well-known *Friedman-Savage hypothesis* are discussed. It is shown that the homogeneous RDU model is consistent with (and in some cases predicts) the simultaneous purchase of lottery tickets and insurance at every (relevant) wealth level without any further assumptions about the shape of the v.Neumann-Morgenstern utility function.

3.1 Risk Aversion in the General Rank-Dependent Utility Model

Let $\succeq$ be a continuous preference relation on $D(X)$ and let the functional $V : D(X) \to \mathbf{R}$ be a representation of this relation. The relation $\succeq$, or alternatively the functional V, is said to display *risk aversion* if $F \succeq G$ or $V(F) \geq V(G)$, respectively, whenever G differs from F by a mean preserving spread. The notion of a *mean preserving spread* can be characterized by the following integral conditions (see [ROTHSCHILD AND STIGLITZ 1970]). The distribution G differs from F by a mean preserving spread if and only if for all $x \in X$

$$\int_0^x (G(t) - F(t))dt \geq 0,$$

and

$$\int_0^M (G(x) - F(x))dx = 0.$$

The notion of *comparative risk aversion* can be defined in terms of simple compensated spreads (see [DIAMOND AND STIGLITZ 1974] and [MACHINA 1982]) which are defined as follows.

Definition 3.1.1 *Let $F, G \in D(X)$; then G is said to differ from F by a simple compensated spread from the point of view of $\succeq$ (or V, respectively,) if $V(G) = V(F)$ and there exists a $x' \in X$ such that $G(x) \geq F(x)$ for $x < x'$ and $G(x) \leq F(x)$ for $x \geq x'$.*

An individual $\succeq$ with corresponding functional V is said to be *more risk averse* than an individual $\succeq^*$ with corresponding functional $V^* : D(X) \to \mathbf{R}$ if $V(F) \geq V(G)$ whenever G differs from F by a simple compensated spread from the point of view of V^*.

It is clear that for an expected value maximizer, i.e. a *risk neutral* individual, every simple compensated spread is a special mean preserving spread. It can be shown that for an expected value maximizer *sequences* of simple compensated spreads are in fact equivalent to mean preserving spreads. Therefore, the relation $\succeq$ displays risk aversion if and only if $\succeq$ is more risk averse than a risk neutral individual in the above sense.

In order to characterize the concepts of risk aversion and comparative risk aversion in the general framework of non-expected utility theory, MACHINA [1982] introduced the notion of *smooth preferences*. He proved that under the assumption that preferences are representable by a *Fréchet differentiable* functional, (global) risk aversion is equivalent to the concavity of every so-called *local utility function* $u_F : X \to \mathbf{R}$. Similarily, an individual described by the functional V is more risk averse than an individual described by V^* if and only if u_F is a concave transform of $(u_F)^*$ for all $F \in D(X)$, provided that both V and V^* are Fréchet differentiable.

Formally, a functional $V : D(X) \to \mathbf{R}$ is said to be Fréchet differentiable at F if there exists a linear functional $\psi(\cdot, F)$ such that

$$\frac{|V(G) - V(F) - \psi(G - F; F)|}{\|G - F\|} \longrightarrow 0$$

whenever $\|G - F\| \to 0$, where $\|\cdot\|$ denotes the L^1 norm. In this case there exists a function u_F, referred to as the local utility function at F, such that

$$V(G) - V(F) = \int_0^M u_F(x)(dG(x) - dF(x)) \; + \; o(\|G - F\|),$$

where $o(\cdot)$ denotes a function which is zero at zero and of higher order than its argument. Note that Fréchet differentiability generalizes the notion of total differentiability of functions with domain in $\mathbf{R}^n$ to functions with domain in a normed vector space.

Consider now the RDU functional $V : D(X) \to \mathbf{R}$ defined by

$$V(F) = \int_0^M v_1(x, 1 - F(x))dx. \tag{3.1}$$

This functional is in general *not* Fréchet differentiable even under the assumptions about the function v which are usually made here. A counterexample can be found in [CHEW, KARNI AND SAFRA 1987]. In the same paper Chew, Karni and Safra showed that Machina's results concerning risk aversion and comparative risk aversion still hold true if the assumption of Fréchet differentiability is relaxed to the weaker assumption of Gâteaux differentiability. It will be shown that the functional V in (3.1) is Gâteaux differentiable if the derivative of v_1 with respect to the second argument, denoted by v_{12}, exists everywhere.

Definition 3.1.2 *For $F, G \in D(X)$ a functional $V : D(X) \to \mathbf{R}$ is weak Gâteaux differentiable at F in direction $(G - F)$ if*

$$\frac{d}{d\theta} V((1-\theta)F + \theta G)\bigg|_{0+} \tag{3.2}$$

exists. The functional V is said to be weak Gâteaux differentiable on $D(X)$ if the expression (3.2) exists throughout $D(X)$ regardless of the direction. Finally, a weakly Gâteaux differentiable V is said to be (strongly) Gâteaux differentiable if there exists a function $u_F : X \to \mathbf{R}$ corresponding to each $F \in D(X)$ such that for every $G \in D(X)$,

$$\frac{d}{d\theta} V((1-\theta)F + \theta G)\bigg|_{0+} = \int_0^M u_F(x)(dG(x) - dF(x)).$$

The function u_F is referred to as the local utility function.

Note that Gâteaux differentiability generalizes the notion of the directional derivative in $\mathbf{R}^n$.

The following lemma states the conditions under which the functional (3.1) is Gâteaux differentiable and gives a simple formula for the local utility function in that case (see also [GREEN AND JULLIEN 1988] where the same formula is given without proof).

Lemma 3.1.3 *The functional V in (3.1) is Gâteaux differentiable if the derivative v_{12} of v_1 with respect to the second argument exists everywhere. In this case the local utility function u_F of V at F is given by*

$$u_F(x) = \int_0^x v_{12}(z, 1 - F(z))dz.$$

Proof. Substituting (3.1) in (3.2) and interchanging integration and differentiation yields

$$\begin{aligned} &\frac{d}{d\theta} V((1-\theta)F + \theta G)\Big|_{0+} \\ &= \int_0^M \frac{d}{d\theta}(v_1(x, 1 - (1-\theta)F(x) - \theta G(x)))\Big|_{0+} dx. \end{aligned}$$

Since v_{12} exists everywhere the right hand side becomes

$$\int_0^M v_{12}(x, 1 - F(x))(F(x) - G(x))dx,$$

which equals

$$-\int_0^M \frac{d}{dx}\left(\int_0^x v_{12}(z, 1 - F(z))dz\right)(G(x) - F(x))dx.$$

Integrating by parts finally yields

$$\begin{aligned} &\frac{d}{d\theta} V((1-\theta)F + \theta G)\Big|_{0+} \\ &= \int_0^M \left(\int_0^x v_{12}(z, 1 - F(z))dz\right)(dG(x) - dF(x)), \end{aligned}$$

and thus the lemma is proved.

We are now ready to give the following characterization theorem of comparative risk aversion for the general RDU model which corresponds to theorem 4 in [GREEN AND JULLIEN 1988].

Theorem 3.1.4 (Green and Jullien) *Let V and V^* be RDU functionals with corresponding generalized utility functions v and v^*, respectively. Assume that v_{12} and v_{12}^* exist everywhere and are differentiable with respect to both arguments. Then V is more risk averse than*

V^* *if and only if for all* $(x,p) \in X \times [0,1]$ *the following two relations hold.*

$$\frac{v_{121}(x,p)}{v_{12}(x,p)} \leq \frac{v^*_{121}(x,p)}{v^*_{12}(x,p)} \tag{3.3}$$

and

$$\frac{v_{122}(x,p)}{v_{12}(x,p)} \geq \frac{v^*_{122}(x,p)}{v^*_{12}(x,p)}. \tag{3.4}$$

Proof. Since a detailed proof can be found in the appendix of [Green and Jullien 1988] it will only be sketched here. Firstly, since V and V^* are Gâteaux differentiable it suffices by the results of Chew, Karni and Safra [1987] to show that for every $F \in D(X)$ the function $x \mapsto \int_0^x v_{12}(z, 1-F(z))dz$ is a concave transform of the function $x \mapsto \int_0^x v^*_{12}(z, 1-F(z))dz$. The relations (3.3) and (3.4) are thus a consequence of Pratt's characterization of concave transforms (see [Pratt 1964]).

Taking in theorem 3.1.4 the functional V^* to be the expectation operator, i.e. $v^*(x,p) = xp$, the following characterization of risk aversion is obtained.

Corollary 3.1.5 *An RDU functional V with corresponding generalized utility function v displays risk aversion in the sense of aversion to any mean preserving spread if and only if on* $X \times [0,1]$

$$v_{121} \leq 0 \quad \textit{and} \quad v_{122} \geq 0.$$

Before the concept of risk aversion will be further analyzed within the framework of the model considered in chapter 2, some immediate applications of theorem 3.1.4 and corollary 3.1.5 are given.

Consider first the case of expected utility theory, i.e. $v(x,p) = u(x)p$. In this case (3.3) reduces to the well-known characterization of comparative risk aversion in terms of the Arrow-Pratt measure of absolute risk aversion $r(x) = -u''(x)/u'(x)$, whereas (3.4) is always satisfied. Also, corollary 3.1.5 yields the equivalence of risk aversion and the concavity of the v.Neumann-Morgenstern utility function.

In the case of anticipated utility theory, i.e. $v(x,p) = u(x)f(p)$ and $v^*(x,p) = u^*(x)f^*(p)$, the relation (3.3) is again the condition $r(x) \geq r^*(x)$ if r^* is the Arrow-Pratt measure corresponding to v^*. The relation (3.4) states in this case that $f''(x)/f'(x) \geq (f^*)''(x)/(f^*)'(x)$ which is equivalent to the condition that f is a convex transform of f^*. Risk aversion in anticipated utility theory is therefore equivalent to the concavity of the utility function u and the convexity of the transformation function f (see also [Chew, Karni and Safra 1987]).

The analysis of risk aversion provided by theorem 3.1.4 and corollary 3.1.5 has an important implication concerning dynamic decision problems. It has been shown in [Green 1987] that in a dynamic context a decision maker whose preferences fail to be quasiconvex can be manipulated in such a way that she would exchange a distribution F for a distribution which is stochastically dominated by F. On the other hand this can never happen if preferences are quasiconvex. It will now be shown that a risk averse RDU maximizer always has quasiconvex preferences.

Theorem 3.1.6 *Let V be an RDU functional with corresponding generalized utility function v which satisfies the hypotheses of theorem 3.1.4 and which displays risk aversion. Then the underlying preference relation is quasiconvex on $D(X)$.*

Proof. We have to show that $G \succeq F$ implies $G \succeq \theta F + (1-\theta)G$ for any $\theta \in [0,1]$. We have

$$\begin{aligned} & V(\theta F + (1-\theta)G) \\ = & \int_0^M v_1(x, 1 - \theta F(x) - (1-\theta)G(x))dx \end{aligned}$$

$$= \int_0^M v_1(x, \theta(1-F(x)) + (1-\theta)(1-G(x)))dx.$$

By corollary 3.1.5, risk aversion implies that v_1 is convex in the second argument, hence

$$\begin{aligned}
&V(\theta F + (1-\theta)G) \\
&\leq \int_0^M \theta v_1(x, 1-F(x)) + (1-\theta)v_1(x, 1-G(x))dx \\
&= \theta \int_0^M v_1(x, 1-F(x))dx + (1-\theta)\int_0^M v_1(x, 1-G(x))dx \\
&= \theta V(F) + (1-\theta)V(G) \\
&\leq \theta V(G) + (1-\theta)V(G) \\
&= V(G).
\end{aligned}$$

The section is concluded with the following observation.

Corollary 3.1.7 *Suppose that an RDU functional displays risk aversion in the sense of corollary 3.1.5. Then the underlying preference relation is quasiconcave if and only if the functional is an expected utility functional.*

Proof. Obviously, preferences are quasiconcave for an expected utility maximizer. Now let conversely $\succeq$ be the underlying preference relation of a risk averse RDU maximizer. By theorem 3.1.6, $\succeq$ is quasiconvex which together with quasiconcavity implies betweenness. Then by lemma 1.4.6 the individual maximizes expected utility.

3.2 Risk Aversion and Homogeneity

In this section it will be proved that an RDU maximizer with a homogeneous generalized utility function can never be averse to *every* mean preserving spread unless the distortion function is constant. On the other hand such an individual can be risk averse in the weaker sense that the certainty equivalent of a distribution is always less than its expectation, i.e. $\delta_{E(F)} \succeq F$ for all $F \in D(X)$. This can be true for a very large class of distortion functions. As noted in the introduction of this chapter, the latter definition of risk aversion is equivalent to the notion of aversion to any mean preserving spread in the case of expected utility theory but differs from it in general non-expected utility theories. For example in the dual theory $\delta_{E(F)} \succeq F$ holds for all $F \in D(X)$ if and only if $h(p) \geq p$ for all $p \in [0,1]$, but aversion to any mean preserving spread is equivalent to the concavity of h (see [RÖELL 1987]).

One of the most interesting features of the dual theory is that – unlike expected utility theory – the dual theory allows to separate the notions of risk aversion and diminishing marginal utility of wealth. Under the expected utility hypothesis both concepts are synonymous since risk aversion is equivalent to the concavity of the v.Neumann-Morgenstern utility function. But it is clear that the notions of risk aversion and diminishing marginal utility of wealth are at a very fundamental level distinct concepts. Thus, the interest in non-expected utility theories arises not only from the descriptive deficiencies of the expected utility model but also from the theoretical desire to conceptually distinguish the notions of risk aversion and diminishing marginal utility of wealth. Since in the dual theory there is no diminishing marginal utility of wealth but there can be risk aversion, the two concepts are kept separate. In the same spirit it will be proved here that the hypothesis of homogeneity in the probabilities is compatible with strict risk aversion in the sense that $\delta_{E(F)} \succ F$ for every non-degenerate $F \in D(X)$ even in the absence of diminishing marginal utility of wealth.

Consider again the general model of section 2.6, i.e. an RDU functional with generalized utility function $v(x,p) = u(x)[f(p)]^{g(x)}$. Recall that we require u and f to be nonnegative and strictly increasing, and $f : [0,1] \to [0,1]$ to be surjective. Furthermore g is a non-increasing, positive function with $(ug)' > 0$ (see assumption 5 in section 2.6). It will be proved now that the hypothesis of aversion to any mean preserving spread implies that g must be constant. Thus, the mean preserving spread concept of risk aversion reduces this model to a special case of the anticipated utility model.

Theorem 3.2.1 *Let V be an RDU functional with generalized utility function $v(x,p) = u(x)[f(p)]^{g(x)}$ satisfying assumption 5 in section 2.6. If g is not constant then there exist distributions F, G such that G is a mean preserving spread of F and $V(G) > V(F)$.*

Proof. By corollary 3.1.5 it suffices to prove that one of the relations $v_{121} \leq 0$ or $v_{122} \geq 0$ fails to hold in the case where g is not constant. It is shown that if $g'(x_0) < 0$ for some $x_0 \in X \setminus \{0\}$ then there will exist probabilities $p \in [0,1]$ such that $v_{121}(x_0, p) > 0$. Differentiation of the function $v : (x,p) \mapsto u(x)[f(p)]^{g(x)}$ with respect to the first variable yields

$$v_1(x,p) = f(p)^{g(x)} \{u'(x) + u(x)g'(x) \ln f(p)\}.$$

The derivative of this expression with respect to the second variable is given by

$$v_{12}(x,p) = f(p)^{g(x)} \frac{f'(p)}{f(p)} \{(ug)'(x) + u(x)g'(x)g(x) \ln f(p)\}.$$

Differentiation again with respect to the first variable yields

$$v_{121}(x,p) = f(p)^{g(x)} \frac{f'(p)}{f(p)} \{(ug)''(x) + \ln f(p) \times$$
$$\left\{2g'(x)(ug)'(x) + g''(x)(ug)(x) + \ln f(p)([g']^2(x)(ug)(x))\right\}\right\}.$$

Thus, if $g'(x_0) < 0$ for some $x_0 \neq 0$ then

$$v_{121}(x_0, p) = \alpha(p)(c_1 + \ln f(p)(c_2 + (\ln f(p))c_3))$$

for a suitable positive function α and a positive constant c_3. But as p tends to zero the term $c_2 + \ln f(p)c_3$ takes arbitrarily large negative values. Therefore the function $p \mapsto v_{121}(x_0, p)/\alpha(p)$ is unbounded and takes arbitrarily large positive values. Hence, there are $p \in [0, 1]$ such that $v_{121}(x_0, p) > 0$.

The just proved theorem calls for some comment. At first sight it might seem surprising that a generalized utility function of the form $v(x,p) = u(x)[f(p)]^{g(x)}$ does not allow for aversion to every mean preserving spread. If for instance $f(p) = p$ and $g > 1$ then, for every fixed x, the transformation function $p \mapsto p^{g(x)}$ is convex. In the anticipated utility model the convexity of the transformation function together with the usual concavity of the utility function u is sufficient for aversion to any mean preserving spread. But as the theorem shows, things are quite different if the transformation function depends on the outcome x. Thus, in the general RDU model the concavity of u and for every fixed x the convexity of the function $p \mapsto v(x,p)$ is *not* sufficient for aversion to every mean preserving spread.

It will now be shown that although an RDU functional with generalized utility function $v(x,p) = u(x)[f(p)]^{g(x)}$ can never display aversion to every mean preserving spread if g is strictly decreasing it can display risk aversion in a weaker sense also in that case. From now on a preference relation on $D(X)$ will be said to display *weak risk aversion* if for all $F \in X$ there is a preference for the sure gain of the expected value $\delta_{E(F)}$ over the distribution F itself.

In the sequel we will concentrate on the properties of the distortion function g that are relevant for weak risk aversion. Therefore, only the case $u(x) = x$ for all $x \in X$ and $f(p) = p$ for $p \in [0, 1]$ will be considered here. Since u is assumed to be the identity, there is no diminishing marginal utility of wealth. The following analysis will show that nevertheless there can be weak risk aversion (even in the strict sense that $\delta_{E(F)} \succ F$ for every non-degenerate $F \in D(X)$).

Thus, in the homogeneous RDU model the notions of diminishing marginal utility of wealth and risk aversion are – at least to some extent – kept separate.

Lemma 3.2.2 *Let $V : D(X) \to \mathbf{R}$ be an RDU functional with a generalized utility function v satisfying $v(x,1) = x$. Then V displays weak risk aversion if on $X \times [0,1]$*

$$v_1(x,p) \leq p.$$

Proof.

$$\begin{aligned} V(\delta_{E(F)}) = v(E(F),1) = E(F) &= \int_0^M (1 - F(x))dx \\ &\geq \int_0^M v_1(x, 1 - F(x))dx \\ &= V(F). \end{aligned}$$

Theorem 3.2.3 *Let V be an RDU functional with generalized utility function $v(x,p) = xp^{g(x)}$. The following two conditions are sufficient for V to display weak risk aversion. For all $x \in X$*

$$g(x) > 1 \tag{3.5}$$

and

$$xg'(x) \geq 1 - g(x). \tag{3.6}$$

Proof. Since $g' \leq 0$, the conditions (3.5) and (3.6) imply

$$0 \leq \frac{xg'(x)}{1 - g(x)} \leq 1.$$

Hence using the inequality $1 + q \leq e^q$ for $q \in \mathbf{R}$ one has

$$1 + \frac{xg'(x)}{1 - g(x)} q \leq e^q$$

for $q \in [0, \infty)$. Substituting $q = (1 - g(x)) \ln p$ yields

$$\begin{aligned} 1 + xg'(x) \ln p &\leq e^{(1-g(x))\ln p} \\ &= p^{1-g(x)}. \end{aligned}$$

Multiplying both sides by $p^{g(x)}$ finally implies $v_1(x,p) \leq p$ for all $(x,p) \in X \times [0,1]$. Thus, by lemma 3.2.2 the generalized utility function $v(x,p) = xp^{g(x)}$ displays weak risk aversion.

The interpretation of the conditions (3.5) and (3.6) which together yield weak risk aversion is as follows. Condition (3.5) guarantees the convexity of the function $p \mapsto p^{g(x)}$ and thus an underestimation of probabilities. Condition (3.6) is a bound for the derivative g'. Roughly, it states that a weakly risk averse individual may not be *too* optimistic towards gambling if prizes become high.

An example of a distortion function g satisfying conditions (3.5) and (3.6) is easy to construct. For simplicity it will be assumed that $M = 1$. It is immediately verified that the function $v(x,p) = xp^{4-x}$ satisfies (3.5), (3.6) and

$$v_1(x,p) < p \tag{3.7}$$

for $p \in (0,1)$. From the proof of lemma 3.2.2 and (3.7) it follows immediately that an RDU maximizer with generalized utility function $v(x,p) = xp^{4-x}$ is weakly risk averse in the strict sense that $\delta_{E(F)} \succ F$ for every non-degenerate distribution $F \in D(X)$.

3.3 Decreasing Risk Aversion

One of the most important hypotheses concerning economic behavior towards risk is the hypothesis that the degree of absolute risk aversion decreases with increasing wealth. In expected utility theory this hypothesis is usually expressed by the assumption that the Arrow-Pratt measure $r(x) = -u''(x)/u'(x)$ is a decreasing function of x, where x

is interpreted as the final wealth position of the decision maker. It follows from theorem 3.1.4 that this assumption is equivalent to the statement that for every $w > 0$ an expected utility maximizer with utility function u is more risk averse than an expected utility maximizer with utility function u^* where $u^*(x) = u(x + w)$.

The criticism of the expected utility model based on the conceptual distinction of risk aversion and diminishing marginal utility of wealth obviously applies also to the characterization of *decreasing* absolute risk aversion in terms of the Arrow-Pratt measure. This is because the Arrow-Pratt measure involves only properties of the utility function u reflecting attitudes towards wealth.

It is interesting to remark that the anticipated utility model is just as vulnerable to this objection as the expected utility model. Unlike the notion of risk aversion which depends in anticipated utility theory on both the utility function u and the transformation function f, the notion of decreasing risk aversion depends in anticipated utility theory – as in the expected utility model – only on the properties of u. This can easily be seen using the characterization of comparative risk aversion given in theorem 3.1.4. An anticipated utility functional with utility function u and transformation function f displays decreasing absolute risk aversion if and only if (3.3) and (3.4) hold for every $w > 0$ and $v(x,p) = u(x)f(p)$, $v^*(x,p) = u(x+w)f(p)$. Thus, the characterization of decreasing risk aversion in anticipated utility theory is exactly the same as in the expected utility model. The reason for this is of course the multiplicative separability of the generalized utility function in the anticipated utility model.

We conclude this section with the observation that in the general RDU model the Arrow-Pratt measure cannot characterize the notion of decreasing risk aversion. To see this, define an individual with generalized utility function v to display decreasing (absolute) risk aversion if for all $w > 0$ the function v^*, given by $v^*(x,p) = v(x + w, p)$ on

$X \times [0,1]$, satisfies (3.3) and (3.4). Then, since the probability transformation function g depends on the wealth position, the example $v(x,p) = u(x)p^{g(x)}$ shows that in RDU theory the notion of decreasing risk aversion involves not only properties of the utility function u but also the way probabilities are perceived.

3.4 The Friedman-Savage Hypothesis

In their classic article, FRIEDMAN and SAVAGE [1948] observed that many individuals were simultaneously purchasing lottery tickets and insurance. In order to explain such behavior they proposed – within the framework of expected utility theory – a v.Neumann-Morgenstern utility function which is concave, hence locally risk averse, about low outcome levels (i.e. low levels of ultimate wealth) and convex, hence locally risk loving, for high outcome levels. There are several difficulties with such an utility function. Firstly, the objection of confusing attitudes towards *risk* and attitudes towards *wealth* again applies to the Friedman-Savage explanation using a S-shaped utility function. Secondly, such an utility function is necessarily unbounded and therefore subject to the criticism stemming from the *St.Petersburg paradox* and its generalizations (see [MENGER 1934/1967]). In light of the latter objection, Friedman and Savage modified their original proposal so as to include a terminal concave section, thus adding a second inflection point. But this modification again raises problems stemming e.g. from the fact that the degree of risk aversion is no longer monotonic with the outcome level (see [MACHINA 1982]).

A further objection to the S-shaped utility function, and also to its modification, is based on the observation that the gambling behavior of individuals is relatively *independent* of current wealth. The simultaneous purchase of lottery tickets and insurance occurs, however, only near the inflection point of an S-shaped utility function. The problems arising from the relative invariance of gambling behavior are discussed in [MACHINA 1982] within the framework of general smooth preferences and in [GREEN AND JULLIEN 1988] within the framework of RDU theory. These authors point out that a bounded preference relation with unbounded local utility functions may explain the invariance of gambling behavior in this context.

Here, it will be shown by means of a simple example that the hypothesis of homogeneity in the probability may predict the simultaneous purchase of lottery tickets and insurance contracts at any relevant wealth level.

In the sequel, preferences are assumed to be defined over $D([0,\infty))$, the space of cumulative distribution functions on $[0,\infty)$. Let $V : D([0,\infty)) \to \mathbf{R}$ be an RDU functional with generalized utility function $v : [0,\infty) \times [0,1] \to \mathbf{R}$. To avoid the difficulties arising eventually from unbounded preferences it is firstly assumed that $u := v(\cdot, 1)$ is bounded. Clearly, this implies that also V is bounded. We will prove now the existence of an arbitrarily large wealth level w_0 such that for *any* wealth level $1 < w < w_0$ and *any* given bounded utility function a homogeneous RDU maximizer will simultaneously buy lottery tickets and insurance contracts provided that the probability distortion function is suitably specified.

The lottery tickets considered here take the following simple form. Any lottery ticket is a fair gamble offering the amount $x_g > 1$ with some probability p_g and 0 otherwise. We will assume lottery tickets to be sold in units at the prize 1. Therefore we may assume $p_g = 1/x_g$.[1] An individual with current wealth $w > 1$ will purchase such a lottery

[1] The assumption that the lottery tickets as well as the insurance contracts below are fair gambles is made here only to simplify the argument. For the results of this section it would suffice to take approximately fair gambles.

ticket if and only if

$$\delta_w \prec (w-1; 1-p_g, w-1+x_g; p_g).$$

Typically, the prize x_g will be fairly high and consequently p_g relatively small.

Insurance contracts are modeled in a similar way. One unit of an insurance is sold at prize 1 and promises to compensate a loss of $x_l > 1$ which occurs with probability $p_l = 1/x_l$. For simplicity it will be assumed that $x_l < w$ so that wealth remains positive in any case. An individual with current wealth w will buy such an insurance contract if and only if

$$\delta_{w-1} \succ (w-x_l; p_l, w; 1-p_l).$$

Theorem 3.4.1 *Let the preferences of an individual be described by an RDU functional* $V : D([0,\infty)) \to \mathbf{R}$ *with generalized utility function* $v(x,p) = u(x)p^{g(x)}$ *where* $u : [0,\infty) \to \mathbf{R}$ *is strictly increasing, bounded and satisfies* $u(0) = 0$. *Furthermore, assume that* $g : [0,\infty) \to \mathbf{R}$ *is positive and strictly decreasing with* $g(x)$ *sufficiently large for small* x *and* $g(x)\ln x \to 0$ *if* $x \to \infty$. *Then the following statements are true.*

(i) *At any wealth level* $w > 1$ *the individual will purchase lottery tickets with sufficiently large prizes.*

(ii) *There exists a* w_0 *such that the individual will insure against large losses at any wealth level* $w < w_0$.

Proof. (i) By formula (2.1) the value of a lottery ticket with prize x_g is given by

$$\begin{aligned} &V((w-1; 1-p_g, w-1+x_g; p_g)) = \\ &\quad u(w-1) + u(w-1+x_g)p_g^{g(w-1+x_g)} - u(w-1)p_g^{g(w-1)}. \end{aligned}$$

Since by assumption $g(x)\ln x \to 0$ for $x \to \infty$ one has for $x_g \to \infty$

$$p_g^{g(w-1+x_g)} = \left(\frac{1}{x_g}\right)^{g(w-1+x_g)} \to 1.$$

Hence, as x_g tends to infinity the value of the corresponding lottery ticket tends to $u(w-1) + u(w-1+x_g) > u(w) = V(\delta_w)$.

(ii) Consider now the case of insurance. The value of no insurance is by (2.1) given as

$$V\left((w - x_l; p_l, w; 1 - p_l)\right) =$$
$$u(w - x_l) + u(w)(1 - p_l)^{g(w)} - u(w - x_l)(1 - p_l)^{g(w-x_l)}.$$

In the extreme case the loss x_l is equal to current wealth w. Then the last expression reduces to the term $u(w)(1-(1/w))^{g(w)}$. If the exponent $g(w)$ is sufficiently large it follows that

$$V(\delta_{w-1}) = u(w-1) > u(w)\left(1 - \frac{1}{w}\right)^{g(w)}.$$

Thus, for any sufficiently large distortion function g there always exists a wealth level w_0 such that an individual with the corresponding homogeneous generalized utility function will at any current wealth level $w < w_0$ insure against the loss of w. By continuity this is also true for losses in a neighborhood of w.

Recall that in theorem 3.2.3 it was proved that $g > 1$ is a crucial property of the distortion function g of an homogeneous RDU functional to display (weak) risk aversion. Thus, the condition $g(x)\ln x \to 0$ if $x \to \infty$ clearly rules out the possibility for an individual to display risk aversion. In contrast, the individual will be risk loving at high outcome levels. On the other hand, the condition of g being sufficiently large for small x guarantees that there is – if not risk aversion – a significant underestimation of probabilities about low outcome levels. Therefore, the conditions in the theorem correspond in a sense to the concavity at low outcomes and convexity at large outcomes in the Friedman-Savage proposal. The specific manner in which the simultaneous purchase of lotteries and insurance is explained, however, is fundamentally different within the two approaches. Whereas Friedman and Savage explain this behavior by a specific attitude towards wealth the same phenomenon is in our approach a consequence of the perception of the relevant probabilities.

As a further remark, we note that the upper bound w_0 in theorem 3.4.1(ii) increases without bound if g increases. Thus, if g is large enough insurances will be purchased at any *relevant* wealth level.

It is also worth noting that the arguments employed in the proof of theorem 3.4.1 do not apply in this form to anticipated utility theory. To demonstrate this consider again the condition for purchasing the lottery tickets. It is immediately verified that an individual which can be represented by an anticipated utility functional will buy a lottery if and only if

$$u(w) < u(w-1) + u(w-1+x_g)f(p_g) - u(w-1)f(p_g),$$

where $f : [0,1] \to [0,1]$ is the corresponding transformation of probabilities. As x_g increases $p_g = 1/x_g$ tends to zero and consequently $f(p_g) \to 0$. Hence, since u is bounded, the right hand side of the above expression converges to $u(w-1) < u(w)$. Thus, an anticipated utility maximizer will not purchase lottery tickets with arbitrarily large outcomes.

There is, however, still a problem with the argument used in theorem 3.4.1. Recall that in the homogeneous RDU model the principle of first-order stochastic dominance requires the product ug to be strictly increasing. But this condition together with $g(x)\ln x \to 0$ for $x \to \infty$ implies that u must be unbounded. There are several possible reactions to this observation.

Firstly, one might be content with violations of first-order stochastic dominance if they occur only at very large outcome levels. Secondly, – and perhaps more convincing – one could give up the requirement of a bounded utility function. In this case the following theorem applies which can be proved in the same way as theorem 3.4.1. Note, however, that the considerations are again restricted to a (sufficiently large) bounded interval $[0, M]$. Also note that there are no assumptions about the shape of the utility function other than unboundedness.

Theorem 3.4.2 *Let $u : [0, M] \to \mathbf{R}$ be any strictly increasing utility function with $u(0) = 0$ and $u(x) \to \infty$ if $x \to M$ and let $w_0 \in (1, M)$. There exists a strictly decreasing, positive function $g : [0, M] \to \mathbf{R}$ such that the product ug is strictly increasing and such that an RDU maximizer with generalized utility function $v(x, p) = u(x)p^{g(x)}$ will exhibit the following behavior.*

(i) *At any wealth level $w \in (1, M)$ the individual will purchase lottery tickets with sufficiently large prizes.*

(ii) *At any wealth level $w < w_0$ the individual will insure against sufficiently large losses.*

Conclusion

Rank-dependent utility (RDU) theory is a model of transitive preferences over probability distributions where the representation of preferences is based upon a (generalized) utility function defined on the outcome/probability-plane. Several specific forms of the generalized utility function have been examined in the literature, all of which imply multiplicative separability in the outcome/probability space. The most general model of this kind is the anticipated utility model firstly introduced in [QUIGGIN 1982]. The anticipated utility model has been proved very useful in explaining much of the empirical evidence against expected utility maximizing behavior.[2]

There are, however, behavioral patterns which can not be modeled in anticipated utility theory. These include the generally observed inclination of many people to participate in gambles promising high prizes with low probabilities. Such a behavior constitutes serious difficulties for the anticipated utility approach – as well as for the expected utility model – especially if accompanied by the simultaneous purchase of insurance contracts. The consequences of this evidence on the expected utility model have been discussed in the classic article of

[2]It is interesting to remark in this context that the anticipated utility model – as a theory of choice under *risk* – corresponds in a precise sense to a recently proposed theory of choice under *uncertainty* generalizing the traditional subjective expected utility model. This model is the theory of *subjective expected utility with non-additive probabilities*, firstly introduced by Schmeidler [1989/1982] and further elaborated by Gilboa [1987] and Wakker [1989]. In Schmeidler's model the subjective "decision weights" derived from "acts" of the decision maker constitute a non-additive probability measure on the states of the world. In anticipated utility theory the decision maker transforms the *given* probabilities in a non-linear way, so that they are finally also treated as non-additive "decision weights". A detailed analysis of the connection between the two approaches can be found in [Wakker 1990a] (see also [Kischka and Puppe 1991]).

FRIEDMAN and SAVAGE [1948]. The solution of the problem proposed by Friedman and Savage is, however, not ultimately convincing. It has been pointed out in [GREEN AND JULLIEN 1988] that also the anticipated utility model can not provide a satisfactory explanation of the simultaneous purchase of lottery tickets and insurance contracts.

Here we have looked for a theory of choice under risk which intrinsically captures an *optimistic* attitude towards gambling, thus explaining the general propensity for gambling. It turned out that the homogeneous version of the RDU model has this property while being consistent with a (weak) concept of risk aversion.

Our main results are the following.

- The general RDU model is best understood as a model where preferences between arbitrary probability distributions are determined by a (generalized) utility function defined on the set of *elementary lotteries.* This set consists of all lotteries with two outcomes one of which is always the "status quo" (section 2.1.3).

- The generalized utility function is – after a simple normalization – unique up to a positive linear transformation, thus a *cardinal* utility on the set of elementary lotteries (section 2.1.1).

- If the corresponding epigraph measure is assumed to be absolutely continuous with respect to the Lebesgue measure the preference relation allows for a very simple representation not only on the set of (finite) lotteries but also on the set of all distribution functions (section 2.1.2).

- The various special cases of the general RDU approach so far considered in the literature may all be characterized by specific forms of the *relative utility index* which reflects the utility of winning a certain amount x with a proportion of the probability

p relative to the utility of winning x with p if otherwise in both cases 0 is received (section 2.5).

- The assumption of the cardinal utility on the set of elementary lotteries being *homogeneous in the probability* corresponds to the case where the relative utility index is independent of the probability (section 2.4).

- Under suitable conditions this assumption is consistent with the axioms of the general RDU approach. In particular, the principle of first-order stochastic dominance implies in this case an *optimistic* attitude towards gambling (section 2.2).

- Homogeneity in the probability yields a plausible explanation of observed behavioral patterns like the *Allais paradox* and the *common ratio effect* (section 2.2).

- The homogeneous RDU model generalizes the expected utility model in a different way than anticipated utility theory does (although there are also RDU theories other than expected utility theory which belong to both approaches). It is also possible to consider a model generalizing both the homogeneous RDU model and anticipated utility theory (section 2.6).

- In general, the homogeneity assumption is incompatible with a strong concept of risk aversion. On the other hand, the homogeneous RDU model shows that a certain kind of optimism towards gambling is consistent with a weaker notion of risk aversion. Thus, an individual which behaves according to the homogeneous RDU model may be simultaneously optimistic *and* risk averse. This can be the case even if there is no diminishing marginal utility of wealth (section 3.2).

- The Arrow-Pratt measure of absolute risk aversion depends in the homogeneous RDU model not only on the properties of the v.Neumann-Morgenstern utility function – as in anticipated utility theory – but also on the function which describes the distortion of the probabilities (section 3.3).

- The fact that in the homogeneous RDU model an individual may display optimism towards gambling and risk aversion at the same time explains and predicts under certain circumstances the simultaneous purchase of lotteries and insurance at any relevant wealth level as required by the *Friedman-Savage hypothesis* (section 3.4).

References

ALLAIS, M. (1953): "Le Comportement de l'Homme Rationnel devant le Risque: Critique des Postulates et Axiomes de l'Ecole Americaine," *Econometrica*, 21, 503–546.

ALLAIS, M. (1979): "The so-called Allais Paradox and Rational Decisions Under Uncertainty," in *Expected Utility Hypotheses and the Allais Paradox*, ed. by M. Allais & O. Hagen. Dordrecht: D. Reidel.

BAUER, H. (1968): *Wahrscheinlichkeitstheorie und Grundzüge der Maßtheorie*, Berlin: de Gruyter.

BELL, D. (1982): "Regret in Decision Making Under Uncertainty," *Operations Research*, 30, 961–981.

BELL, D. (1985): "Disappointment in Decision Making Under Uncertainty," *Operations Research*, 33, 1–27.

BERNOULLI, D. (1738/1954): "Specimen Theoriae Novae de Mensura Sortis," *Commentarii Academiae Scientarum Imperialis Petropolitanae*, 5, 175–192. English translation: *Econometrica* (1954), 22, 23–36.

CHATEAUNEUF, A. (1990): "On the Use of Comonotonicity in the Axiomatization of EURDP Theory for Arbitrary Consequences," Paper presented at the V.International Conference on the Foundations and Application of Utility, Risk and Decision Theories, Duke University, North Carolina.

CHEW, S. H. (1983): "A Generalization of the Quasilinear Mean with Applications to the Measurement of Income Inequality and Decision Theory Resolving the Allais Paradox," *Econometrica*, 51, 1065–1092.

CHEW, S. H. (1985): "Implicit Weighted and Semi-Weighted Utility Theories, M-Estimators and the Non-Demand Revelation of Second-Prize Auctions for an Uncertain Auctioned Object," Working Paper # 155, Johns Hopkins University.

CHEW, S. H. (1989a): "Axiomatic Utility Theories with the Betweenness Property," *Annals of Operations Research*, 19, 273–298.

CHEW, S. H. (1989b): "An Axiomatic Generalization of the Quasilinear Mean and Gini Mean with Application to Decision Theory," Johns Hopkins University and Tulane University; rewritten version of "An Axiomatization of the Rank-Dependent Quasilinear Mean Generalizing the Gini Mean and the Quasilinear Mean," (1985), Working Paper # 156, Johns Hopkins University.

CHEW, S. H., AND L. EPSTEIN (1989): "A Unifying Approach to Axiomatic Non-Expected Utility Theories," *Journal of Economic Theory*, 49, 207–240.

CHEW, S. H., E. KARNI, AND Z. SAFRA (1987): "Risk Aversion in the Theory of Expected Utility with Rank-Dependent Probabilities," *Journal of Economic Theory*, 42, 370–381.

CHEW, S. H., W. S. WALLER (1986): "Empirical Tests of Weighted Utility Theory," *Journal of Mathematical Psychology*, 30, 55–72.

DEBREU, G. (1964): "Continuity Properties of Paretian Utility," *International Economic Review*, 5, 285–293.

DEKEL, E. (1986): "An Axiomatic Characterization of Preferences Under Uncertainty: Weakening the Independence Axiom," *Journal of Economic Theory*, 40, 304–318.

DIAMOND, P. A., AND J. E. STIGLITZ (1974): "Increases in Risk and in Risk Aversion," *Journal of Economic Theory*, 8, 337–360.

EDWARDS, W. (1955): "The Prediction of Decisions Among Bets," *Journal of Experimental Psychology*, 50, 201–214.

EDWARDS, W. (1962): "Subjective Probabilities Inferred from Decisions," *Psychological Review*, 69, 109–135.

EICHHORN, W. (1978): *Functional Equations in Economics.* London: Addison-Wesley.

ELLSBERG, D. (1961): "Risk, Ambiguity, and the Savage Axioms," *Quarterly Journal of Economics*, 75, 643–669.

FELLNER, W. (1961): "Distortion of Subjective Probabilities as a Reaction to Uncertainty," *Quarterly Journal of Economics*, 75, 670–689.

FISHBURN, P. C. (1978): "On Handa's 'New Theory of Cardinal Utility' and the Maximization of Expected Return", *Journal of Political Economy*, 86, 321–324.

FISHBURN, P. C. (1982): "Nontransitive Measurable Utility," *Journal of Mathematical Psychology*, 26, 31–67.

FISHBURN, P. C. (1983): "Transitive Measurable Utility," *Journal of Economic Theory*, 31, 293–317.

FISHBURN, P. C. (1984a): "SSB Utility Theory: An Economic Perspective," *Mathematical Social Sciences*, 8, 63–94.

FISHBURN, P. C. (1984b): "SSB Utility Theory and Decision-Making under Uncertainty," *Mathematical Social Sciences*, 8, 253–285.

FISHBURN, P. C. (1986a): "A New Model for Decisions Under Uncertainty," *Economics Letters*, 21, 127–130.

FISHBURN, P. C. (1986b): "Implicit Mean Value and Certainty Equivalence," *Econometrica*, 54, 1197–1205.

FISHBURN, P. C. (1988): *Nonlinear Preference and Utility Theory.* Baltimore: The Johns Hopkins University Press.

FISHBURN, P. C., AND I. H. LAVALLE (1987): "A Nonlinear, Nontransitive and Additive-Probability Model for Decisions Under Uncertainty," *Annals of Statistics*, 15, 830–844.

FRIEDMAN, M., AND L. J. SAVAGE (1948): "The Utility Analysis of Choices Involving Risk," *Journal of Political Economy*, 56, 279–304.

GILBOA, I. (1987): "Expected Utility with Purely Subjective Non-Additive Probabilities," *Journal of Mathematical Economics*, 16, 65–88.

GRANDMONT, J. M. (1972): "Continuity Properties of v.Neumann-Morgenstern Utility," *Journal of Economic Theory*, 4, 45–57.

GREEN, J. R. (1987): "Making Book Against Oneself, The Independence Axiom, and Nonlinear Utility Theory," *Quarterly Journal of Economics*, 98, 785–796.

GREEN, J. R., AND B. JULLIEN (1988): "Ordinal Independence in Nonlinear Utility Theory," *Journal of Risk and Uncertainty*, 1, 355–387.

Grether, D. M., and C. Plott (1979): "Economic Theory of Choice and the Preference Reversal Phenomenon," *American Economic Review*, 69, 623–638.

Hadar, J., and W. Russell (1969): "Rules for Ordering Uncertain Prospects," *American Economic Review*, 59, 25–34.

Handa, J. (1977): "Risk, Probabilities and a New Theory of Cardinal Utility," *Journal of Political Economy*, 85, 97–122.

Hazen, G. (1987): "Subjectively Weighted Linear Utility," *Theory and Decision*, 23, 25–78.

Herstein, I., and J. Milnor (1953): "An Axiomatic Approach to Measurable Utility," *Econometrica*, 21, 291–297.

Holt, C. A. (1986): "Preference Reversals and the Independence Axiom," *American Economic Review*, 76, 508–515.

Jorland, G. (1987): "The Saint Petersburg Paradox 1713–1937," in *The Probabilistic Revolution, Volume I: Ideas in History*, ed. by L. Krüger, L. J. Daston & M. Heidelberger. Cambridge, Massachusetts: MIT Press.

Kahneman, D., and A. Tversky (1979): "Prospect Theory: An Analysis of Decision Under Risk," *Econometrica*, 47, 263–291.

Karmarkar, U. S. (1978): "Subjectively Weighted Utility: A Descriptive Extension of the Expected Utility Model," *Organizational Behavior and Human Performance*, 21, 61–72.

Karni, E., and Z. Safra (1987): "'Preference Reversal' and the Observability of Preferences by Experimental Methods," *Econometrica*, 55, 675–685.

KARNI, E., AND D. SCHMEIDLER (1990): "Utility Theory with Uncertainty," in *Handbook of Mathematical Economics*, ed. by W. Hildenbrand & H. Sonnenschein. North Holland, forthcoming.

KISCHKA, P., AND C. PUPPE (1991): "Decisions Under Risk and Uncertainty: A Survey of Recent Developments," *Zeitschrift für Operations Research*, forthcoming.

LICHTENSTEIN, S., AND P. SLOVIC (1971): "Reversals of Preferences Between Bids and Choices in Gambling Decisions," *Journal of Experimental Psychology*, 89, 46–55.

LICHTENSTEIN, S., AND P. SLOVIC (1973): "Response-Induced Reversals of Preference in Gambling: An Extended Replication in Las Vegas," *Journal of Experimental Psychology*, 101, 16–20.

LOOMES, G., AND R. SUGDEN (1982): "Regret Theory: An Alternative Theory of Rational Choice Under Uncertainty," *Economic Journal*, 92, 805–824.

LOOMES, G., AND R. SUGDEN (1987): "Some Implications of a More General Form of Regret Theory," *Journal of Economic Theory*, 41, 270–287.

MACCRIMMON, K. R. (1968): "Descriptive and Normative Implications of the Decision-Theory Postulates," in *Risk and Uncertainty: Proceedings of a Conference Held by the International Economic Association*, ed. by K. H. Borch & J. Mossin. London: Macmillan.

MACCRIMMON, K.R., AND S. LARSSON (1979): "Utility Theory: Axioms Versus 'Paradoxes'," in *Expected Utility Hypotheses and the Allais Paradox*, ed. by M. Allais & O. Hagen. Dordrecht: D. Reidel.

Machina, M. (1982): "'Expected Utility' Analysis Without the Independence Axiom," *Econometrica*, 50, 277–323.

Machina, M. (1987): "Choice Under Uncertainty: Problems Solved and Unsolved," *Journal of Economic Perspectives*, 1, 127–154.

Menger, K. (1934/1967): "The Role of Uncertainty in Economics," in *Essays in Mathematical Economics in Honor of Oskar Morgenstern*, ed. by M. Shubik. Princeton: Princeton University Press, 1967. Translated from *Zeitschrift für Nationalökonomie*, Band V, Heft 4, 1934, 459–485.

Natanson, I. P. (1961): *Theorie der Funktionen einer reellen Veränderlichen.* Berlin: Akademie Verlag.

Pratt, J. W. (1964): "Risk Aversion in the Small and in the Large," *Econometrica*, 32, 122–136.

Preston, M., and P. Baratta (1948): "An Experimental Study of the Auction-Value of an Uncertain Outcome," *American Journal of Psychology*, 61, 183–193.

Puppe, C. (1990a): "Preference Functionals With Prize-Dependent Distortions of Probabilities," *Economics Letters*, 33, 127–131.

Puppe, C. (1990b): "The Irrelevance Axiom, Relative Utility and Choice Under Risk," Working Paper 4/90, Universität Karlsruhe.

Puppe, C. (1990c): "Reduction of Decision Problems: Some Remarks on Rank-Dependent Utility Theory," Paper presented at the VI.World Congress of the Econometric Society, Barcelona.

Quiggin, J. (1982): "A Theory of Anticipated Utility," *Journal of Economic Behavior and Organization*, 3, 323–343.

RAIFFA, H. (1961): "Risk, Ambiguity, and the Savage Axioms," *Quarterly Journal of Economics*, 75, 690–694.

RÖELL, A. (1987): "Risk Aversion in Quiggin and Yaari's Rank-Order Model of Choice Under Uncertainty," *Economic Journal*, 97, Supplement, 143–159.

ROTHSCHILD, M., AND J. E. STIGLITZ (1970): "Increasing Risk: I. A Definition," *Journal of Economic Theory*, 2, 225–243.

ROYDEN, H. L. (1968): *Real Analysis.* London: Macmillan, Second edition.

SAVAGE, L. J. (1954): *The Foundations of Statistics*, New York: Wiley.

SCHMEIDLER, D. (1989): "Subjective Probability and Expected Utility Without Additivity," *Econometrica*, 57, 571–587; first version: 1982.

SCHNEEWEISS, H. (1967): *Entscheidungskriterien bei Risiko*, Berlin – Heidelberg: Springer.

SEGAL, U. (1984): "Nonlinear Decision Weights with the Independence Axiom," UCLA Working Paper # 353.

SEGAL, U. (1987a): "Some Remarks on Quiggin's Anticipated Utility," *Journal of Economic Behavior and Organization*, 8, 145–154.

SEGAL, U. (1987b): "The Ellsberg Paradox and Risk Aversion: An Anticipated Utility Approach," *International Economic Review*, 28,175–202.

SEGAL, U. (1989): "Anticipated Utility Theory: A Measure Representation Approach," *Annals of Operations Research*, 19, 359–373.

SEGAL, U. (1990): "Two-Stage Lotteries Without the Reduction Axiom," *Econometrica*, 58, 349–379.

SLOVIC, P., AND A. TVERSKY (1974): "Who Accepts Savage's Axiom?," *Behavioral Science*, 19, 368–373.

VON NEUMANN, J., AND O. MORGENSTERN (1947): *Theory of Games and Economic Behavior*, Princeton: Princeton University Press, Second edition.

WAKKER, P. (1989): *Additive Representations of Preferences*, Dordrecht: Kluwer.

WAKKER, P. (1990a): "Under Stochastic Dominance Choquet-Expected Utility and Anticipated Utility are Identical," *Theory and Decision*, forthcoming.

WAKKER, P. (1990b): "Additive Representations of Preferences on Rank-Ordered Subsets of Cartesian Products; Part I: The Algebraic Approach, Part II: The Topological Approach," Working Papers # 9001, 9002, Duke University, Fuqua School of Business.

WEBER, M., AND C. CAMERER (1987): "Recent Developments in Modelling Preferences Under Risk," *OR Spektrum*, 9, 129–151.

YAARI, M. (1987): "The Dual Theory of Choice Under Risk," *Econometrica*, 55, 95–115.

Vol. 261: Th.R.Gulledge, Jr., N.K. Womer, The Economics of Made-to-Order Production. VI, 134 pages. 1986.

Vol. 262: H.U. Buhl, A Neo-Classical Theory of Distribution and Wealth. V, 146 pages. 1986.

Vol. 263: M. Schäfer, Resource Extraction and Market Structure. XI, 154 pages. 1986.

Vol. 264: Models of Economic Dynamics. Proceedings, 1983. Edited by H.F. Sonnenschein. VII, 212 pages. 1986.

Vol. 265: Dynamic Games and Applications in Economics. Edited by T. Başar. IX, 288 pages. 1986.

Vol. 266: Multi-Stage Production Planning and Inventory Control. Edited by S. Axsäter, Ch. Schneeweiss and E. Silver. V, 264 pages. 1986.

Vol. 267: R. Bemelmans, The Capacity Aspect of Inventories. IX, 165 pages. 1986.

Vol. 268: V. Firchau, Information Evaluation in Capital Markets. VII, 103 pages. 1986.

Vol. 269: A. Borglin, H. Keiding, Optimality in Infinite Horizon Economies. VI, 180 pages. 1986.

Vol. 270: Technological Change, Employment and Spatial Dynamics. Proceedings 1985. Edited by P. Nijkamp. VII, 466 pages. 1986.

Vol. 271: C. Hildreth, The Cowles Commission in Chicago, 1939–1955. V, 176 pages. 1986.

Vol. 272: G. Clemenz, Credit Markets with Asymmetric Information. VIII, 212 pages. 1986.

Vol. 273: Large-Scale Modelling and Interactive Decision Analysis. Proceedings, 1985. Edited by G. Fandel, M. Grauer, A. Kurzhanski and A.P. Wierzbicki. VII, 363 pages. 1986.

Vol. 274: W.K. Klein Haneveld, Duality in Stochastic Linear and Dynamic Programming. VII, 295 pages. 1986.

Vol. 275: Competition, Instability, and Nonlinear Cycles. Proceedings, 1985. Edited by W. Semmler. XII, 340 pages. 1986.

Vol. 276: M.R. Baye, D.A. Black, Consumer Behavior, Cost of Living Measures, and the Income Tax. VII, 119 pages. 1986.

Vol. 277: Studies in Austrian Capital Theory, Investment and Time. Edited by M. Faber. VI, 317 pages. 1986.

Vol. 278: W.E. Diewert, The Measurement of the Economic Benefits of Infrastructure Services. V, 202 pages. 1986.

Vol. 279: H.-J. Büttler, G. Frei and B. Schips, Estimation of Disequilibrium Models. VI, 114 pages. 1986.

Vol. 280: H.T. Lau, Combinatorial Heuristic Algorithms with FORTRAN. VII, 126 pages. 1986.

Vol. 281: Ch.-L. Hwang, M.-J. Lin, Group Decision Making under Multiple Criteria. XI, 400 pages. 1987.

Vol. 282: K. Schittkowski, More Test Examples for Nonlinear Programming Codes. V, 261 pages. 1987.

Vol. 283: G. Gabisch, H.-W. Lorenz, Business Cycle Theory. VII, 229 pages. 1987.

Vol. 284: H. Lütkepohl, Forecasting Aggregated Vector ARMA Processes. X, 323 pages. 1987.

Vol. 285: Toward Interactive and Intelligent Decision Support Systems. Volume 1. Proceedings, 1986. Edited by Y. Sawaragi, K. Inoue and H. Nakayama. XII, 445 pages. 1987.

Vol. 286: Toward Interactive and Intelligent Decision Support Systems. Volume 2. Proceedings, 1986. Edited by Y. Sawaragi, K. Inoue and H. Nakayama. XII, 450 pages. 1987.

Vol. 287: Dynamical Systems. Proceedings, 1985. Edited by A.B. Kurzhanski and K. Sigmund. VI, 215 pages. 1987.

Vol. 288: G.D. Rudebusch, The Estimation of Macroeconomic Disequilibrium Models with Regime Classification Information. VII, 128 pages. 1987.

Vol. 289: B.R. Meijboom, Planning in Decentralized Firms. X, 168 pages. 1987.

Vol. 290: D.A. Carlson, A. Haurie, Infinite Horizon Optimal Control. XI, 254 pages. 1987.

Vol. 291: N. Takahashi, Design of Adaptive Organizations. VI, 140 pages. 1987.

Vol. 292: I. Tchijov, L. Tomaszewicz (Eds.), Input-Output Modeling. Proceedings, 1985. VI, 195 pages. 1987.

Vol. 293: D. Batten, J. Casti, B. Johansson (Eds.), Economic Evolution and Structural Adjustment. Proceedings, 1985. VI, 382 pages. 1987.

Vol. 294: J. Jahn, W. Krabs (Eds.), Recent Advances and Historical Development of Vector Optimization. VII, 405 pages. 1987.

Vol. 295: H. Meister, The Purification Problem for Constrained Games with Incomplete Information. X, 127 pages. 1987.

Vol. 296: A. Börsch-Supan, Econometric Analysis of Discrete Choice. VIII, 211 pages. 1987.

Vol. 297: V. Fedorov, H. Läuter (Eds.), Model-Oriented Data Analysis. Proceedings, 1987. VI, 239 pages. 1988.

Vol. 298: S.H. Chew, Q. Zheng, Integral Global Optimization. VII, 179 pages. 1988.

Vol. 299: K. Marti, Descent Directions and Efficient Solutions in Discretely Distributed Stochastic Programs. XIV, 178 pages. 1988.

Vol. 300: U. Derigs, Programming in Networks and Graphs. XI, 315 pages. 1988.

Vol. 301: J. Kacprzyk, M. Roubens (Eds.), Non-Conventional Preference Relations in Decision Making. VII, 155 pages. 1988.

Vol. 302: H.A. Eiselt, G. Pederzoli (Eds.), Advances in Optimization and Control. Proceedings, 1986. VIII, 372 pages. 1988.

Vol. 303: F.X. Diebold, Empirical Modeling of Exchange Rate Dynamics. VII, 143 pages. 1988.

Vol. 304: A. Kurzhanski, K. Neumann, D. Pallaschke (Eds.), Optimization, Parallel Processing and Applications. Proceedings, 1987. VI, 292 pages. 1988.

Vol. 305: G.-J.C.Th. van Schijndel, Dynamic Firm and Investor Behaviour under Progressive Personal Taxation. X, 215 pages. 1988.

Vol. 306: Ch. Klein, A Static Microeconomic Model of Pure Competition. VIII, 139 pages. 1988.

Vol. 307: T.K. Dijkstra (Ed.), On Model Uncertainty and its Statistical Implications. VII, 138 pages. 1988.

Vol. 308: J.R. Daduna, A. Wren (Eds.), Computer-Aided Transit Scheduling. VIII, 339 pages. 1988.

Vol. 309: G. Ricci, K. Velupillai (Eds.), Growth Cycles and Multisectoral Economics: the Goodwin Tradition. III, 126 pages. 1988.

Vol. 310: J. Kacprzyk, M. Fedrizzi (Eds.), Combining Fuzzy Imprecision with Probabilistic Uncertainty in Decision Making. IX, 399 pages. 1988.

Vol. 311: R. Färe, Fundamentals of Production Theory. IX, 163 pages. 1988.

Vol. 312: J. Krishnakumar, Estimation of Simultaneous Equation Models with Error Components Structure. X, 357 pages. 1988.

Vol. 313: W. Jammernegg, Sequential Binary Investment Decisions. VI, 156 pages. 1988.

Vol. 314: R. Tietz, W. Albers, R. Selten (Eds.), Bounded Rational Behavior in Experimental Games and Markets. VI, 368 pages. 1988.

Vol. 315: I. Orishimo, G.J.D. Hewings, P. Nijkamp (Eds.), Information Technology: Social and Spatial Perspectives. Proceedings, 1986. VI, 268 pages. 1988.

Vol. 316: R.L. Basmann, D.J. Slottje, K. Hayes, J.D. Johnson, D.J. Molina, The Generalized Fechner-Thurstone Direct Utility Function and Some of its Uses. VIII, 159 pages. 1988.

Vol. 317: L. Bianco, A. La Bella (Eds.), Freight Transport Planning and Logistics. Proceedings, 1987. X, 568 pages. 1988.

Vol. 318: T. Doup, Simplicial Algorithms on the Simplotope. VIII, 262 pages. 1988.

Vol. 319: D.T. Luc, Theory of Vector Optimization. VIII, 173 pages. 1989.

Vol. 320: D. van der Wijst, Financial Structure in Small Business. VII, 181 pages. 1989.

Vol. 321: M. Di Matteo, R.M. Goodwin, A. Vercelli (Eds.), Technological and Social Factors in Long Term Fluctuations. Proceedings. IX, 442 pages. 1989.

Vol. 322: T. Kollintzas (Ed.), The Rational Expectations Equilibrium Inventory Model. XI, 269 pages. 1989.

Vol. 323: M.B.M. de Koster, Capacity Oriented Analysis and Design of Production Systems. XII, 245 pages. 1989.

Vol. 324: I.M. Bomze, B.M. Pötscher, Game Theoretical Foundations of Evolutionary Stability. VI, 145 pages. 1989.

Vol. 325: P. Ferri, E. Greenberg, The Labor Market and Business Cycle Theories. X, 183 pages. 1989.

Vol. 326: Ch. Sauer, Alternative Theories of Output, Unemployment, and Inflation in Germany: 1960–1985. XIII, 206 pages. 1989.

Vol. 327: M. Tawada, Production Structure and International Trade. V, 132 pages. 1989.

Vol. 328: W. Güth, B. Kalkofen, Unique Solutions for Strategic Games. VII, 200 pages. 1989.

Vol. 329: G. Tillmann, Equity, Incentives, and Taxation. VI, 132 pages. 1989.

Vol. 330: P.M. Kort, Optimal Dynamic Investment Policies of a Value Maximizing Firm. VII, 185 pages. 1989.

Vol. 331: A. Lewandowski, A.P. Wierzbicki (Eds.), Aspiration Based Decision Support Systems. X, 400 pages. 1989.

Vol. 332: T.R. Gulledge, Jr., L.A. Litteral (Eds.), Cost Analysis Applications of Economics and Operations Research. Proceedings. VII, 422 pages. 1989.

Vol. 333: N. Dellaert, Production to Order. VII, 158 pages. 1989.

Vol. 334: H.-W. Lorenz, Nonlinear Dynamical Economics and Chaotic Motion. XI, 248 pages. 1989.

Vol. 335: A. G. Lockett, G. Islei (Eds.), Improving Decision Making in Organisations. Proceedings. IX, 606 pages. 1989.

Vol. 336: T. Puu, Nonlinear Economic Dynamics. VII, 119 pages. 1989.

Vol. 337: A. Lewandowski, I. Stanchev (Eds.), Methodology and Software for Interactive Decision Support. VIII, 309 pages. 1989.

Vol. 338: J.K. Ho, R.P. Sundarraj, DECOMP: an Implementation of Dantzig-Wolfe Decomposition for Linear Programming. VI, 206 pages. 1989.

Vol. 339: J. Terceiro Lomba, Estimation of Dynamic Econometric Models with Errors in Variables. VIII, 116 pages. 1990.

Vol. 340: T. Vasko, R. Ayres, L. Fontvieille (Eds.), Life Cycles and Long Waves. XIV, 293 pages. 1990.

Vol. 341: G.R. Uhlich, Descriptive Theories of Bargaining. IX, 165 pages. 1990.

Vol. 342: K. Okuguchi, F. Szidarovszky, The Theory of Oligopoly with Multi-Product Firms. V, 167 pages. 1990.

Vol. 343: C. Chiarella, The Elements of a Nonlinear Theory of Economic Dynamics. IX, 149 pages. 1990.

Vol. 344: K. Neumann, Stochastic Project Networks. XI, 237 pages. 1990.

Vol. 345: A. Cambini, E. Castagnoli, L. Martein, P. Mazzoleni, S. Schaible (Eds.), Generalized Convexity and Fractional Programming with Economic Applications. Proceedings, 1988. VII, 361 pages. 1990.

Vol. 346: R. von Randow (Ed.), Integer Programming and Related Areas. A Classified Bibliography 1984–1987. XIII, 514 pages. 1990.

Vol. 347: D. Ríos Insua, Sensitivity Analysis in Multi-objective Decision Making. XI, 193 pages. 1990.

Vol. 348: H. Störmer, Binary Functions and their Applications. VIII, 151 pages. 1990.

Vol. 349: G. A. Pfann, Dynamic Modelling of Stochastic Demand for Manufacturing Employment. VI, 158 pages. 1990.

Vol. 350: W.-B. Zhang, Economic Dynamics. X, 232 pages. 1990.

Vol. 351: A. Lewandowski, V. Volkovich (Eds.), Multiobjective Problems of Mathematical Programming. Proceedings, 1988. VII, 315 pages. 1991.

Vol. 352: O. van Hilten, Optimal Firm Behaviour in the Context of Technological Progress and a Business Cycle. XII, 229 pages. 1991.

Vol. 353: G. Ricci (Ed.), Decision Processes in Economics. Proceedings, 1989. III, 209 pages. 1991.

Vol. 354: M. Ivaldi, A Structural Analysis of Expectation Formation. XII, 230 pages. 1991.

Vol. 355: M. Salomon, Deterministic Lotsizing Models for Production Planning. VII, 158 pages. 1991.

Vol. 356: P. Korhonen, A. Lewandowski, J. Wallenius (Eds.), Multiple Criteria Decision Support. Proceedings, 1989. XII, 393 pages. 1991.

Vol. 358: P. Knottnerus, Linear Models with Correlated Disturbances. VIII, 196 pages. 1991.

Vol. 359: E. de Jong, Exchange Rate Determination and Optimal Economic Policy Under Various Exchange Rate Regimes. VII, 270 pages. 1991.

Vol. 360: P. Stalder, Regime Transitions, Spillovers and Buffer Stocks. VI, 193 pages. 1991.

Vol. 361: C. F. Daganzo, Logistics Systems Analysis. X, 321 pages. 1991.

Vol. 362: F. Gehrels, Essays in Macroeconomics of an Open Economy. VII, 183 pages. 1991.

Vol. 363: C. Puppe, Distorted Probabilities and Choice under Risk. VIII, 100 pages. 1991.